The Homebrewed Christianity
Guide to the End Times

The Homebrewed Christianity Guide to the End Times

Theology After You've Been Left Behind

JEFFREY C. PUGH
AUTHOR

TRIPP FULLER
SERIES EDITOR

Fortress Press
Minneapolis

THE HOMEBREWED CHRISTIANITY GUIDE TO
THE END TIMES
Theology After You've Been Left Behind

Cover design: Jesse Turri
Book design: PerfecType, Nashville, TN

Library of Congress Cataloging-in-Publication Data
Print ISBN: 978-1-4514-9954-4
eBook ISBN: 978-1-5064-0143-0

The paper used in this publication meets the minimum
requirements of American National Standard for Information Sciences—Permanence of Paper for Printed Library
Materials, ANSI Z329.48-1984.

Manufactured in the U.S.A.

For Benjamin, Anna Grace, Campbell, and Alayna

The future is in your hands

Contents

Series Introduction

You are about to read a guidebook. Not only is the book the sweet "guide book" size, shaped perfectly to take a ride in your back pocket, but the book itself was crafted with care by a real-deal theology nerd. Here's the thing. The Homebrewed Christianity Guide series has one real goal: we want to think *with* you, not *for* you.

The whole "homebrew" metaphor grows from my passion for helping anyone who wants to geek out about theology to do so with the best ingredients around. That's why I started the Homebrewed Christianity podcast in 2008, and that's why I am thrilled to partner with Fortress Press's Theology for the People team to produce this series. I am confident that the church has plenty of intelligent and passionate people who want a more robust conversation about their faith.

A podcast, in case you're wondering, is like talk radio on demand without the commercials. You download a file and listen when, if, where, and how long you want. I love the podcast medium. Short of talking one-on-one, there's hardly a more intimate presence than speaking to someone in their earbuds as they're stuck in traffic, on the treadmill, or washing dishes. When I started the podcast,

I wanted to give anyone the option of listening to some of the best thinkers from the church and the academy.

Originally, the podcast was for friends, family, and my local pub theology group. I figured people in the group were more likely to listen to a podcast than read a giant book. So as the resident theology nerd, I read the books and then interviewed the authors. Soon, thousands of people were listening. Since then the audience has grown to over fifty thousand unique listeners each month and over a million downloads. A community of listeners, whom we call Deacons, grew, and we've got a cast of co-hosts and regular guests.

Over the better part of a decade, I have talked to scores of theologians and engaged with the Deacons about these conversations. It has been a real joy. Every time I hear from a listener, I do the happy dance in my soul.

And here's the deal: I love theology, but I love the church more. I am convinced that the church can really make a difference in the world. But in order to do that, it needs to face reality rather than run from it. The church must use its brain, live its faith, and join God in working for the salvation of the world. And that's what these books are all about.

We often open and close the podcast by reminding listeners that we are providing the ingredients so that they can brew their own faith. That's the same with these books. Each author is an expert theological brewer, and they've been asked to write from their own point of view. These guidebooks are not boringly neutral; instead, they are zestily provocative, meant to get you thinking and brewing.

I look forward to hearing from you on the Speakpipe at HomebrewedChristianity.com and meeting you at an HBC 3D event. We can drink a pint and talk about this book, how you agree and disagree with it. Because if we're talking about theology, the world is a better place.

And remember: Share the Brew!

Tripp Fuller

The Homebrewed Posse

Whether it's the podcast, the blog, or live events, Homebrewed Christianity has always been a conversation, and these books are no different. So inside of this and every volume in the HBC book, you'll be hearing from four members of the Homebrewed community. They are:

THE BISHOP

The Bishop: Kindly, pastoral, encouraging. She's been around the block a few times, and nothing ruffles her feathers. She wants everyone to succeed, and she's an optimist, so she knows they will.

THE ELDER

The Elder: Scolding, arrogant, know-it-all. He's old and disgruntled, the father figure you can never please. He loves quoting doctrine; he's the kind of guy who controls every church meeting because he knows Roberts Rules of Order better than anyone else.

THE DEACON

The Deacon: Earnest, excited, energetic. He's a guy who has just discovered HBC, and he can't get enough of it. He's a cheerleader, a shouter, an encourager. He's still in his first naïveté.

THE ACOLYTE

The Acolyte: Smart, inquisitive, skeptical. She's the smartest student in your confirmation class. She's bound to be a biologist or a physicist, and she's skeptical of all the hocus pocus of Christianity. But she hasn't given up on it yet, so her questions come from the heart. She really wants to know if all this stuff works.

We look forward to continuing the conversation with you, online and in-person!

Preface

When Tony Jones and Tripp Fuller first sat down with me to ask if I was interested in writing a book for the Homebrewed Guides to Christianity, I was intrigued. I love the Homebrewed podcasts; they explore the most interesting theology today. But the more they talked the more anxious I became:

"We want these books to be written for a general audience, not to academic ones."

"But, I can have footnotes, right?"

"Well, maybe, but can you keep them to a minimum, and even then can you make them like David Foster Wallace's, you know, witty and intelligent?"

"Wait, I have to be intelligent?"

"Well, it's preferable, but can you at least be funny?"

"Funny? I've got to be funny?"

"Look dude, we're going for the Jon Stewart crowd here, the Stephen Colbert demographic. If you could make it a little snarky, that'd be a big plus for us."

"Okay, so, you want funny, snarky theology that should be intelligent and challenging for your readers? That about cover it?"

"Pretty much . . . oh, one more thing—can you make it short? We want these books to fit in the back pocket of jeans so people can read them on subways and buses. The good news is that we have a lot of topics still open."

"Cool, can I have Jesus?"

"No, Tripp took that one already; he got first choice. But we have a long list: evil, sin, church history, holy spirit, end times—"

"Stop! Did you say end times? Cool, I'm in."

Maybe it was the happy vibes that you get at the AAR/SBL Fortress receptions, but I found myself agreeing to do this book on the spot. However, on the walk back to my hotel room those familiar inner voices of reflection started their clamoring for attention.

"This sounds like it could be fun. Snarky theology. It's a whole new genre, right up your alley."

"Really? You think this'll be fun? People read these books, you know. Don't trifle with this; you'll ruin your reputation. Do you really want to be known as the Zach Galifianakis of theology?"

"Seriously? That would be awesome!"

Once the screeching laughter stopped drowning out the calliope music usually playing in my head, I stopped and laughed. I suspect that I wasn't alone when the other authors were working this through (except for Tripp; I'm pretty sure Tripp's game for anything). These guides are supposed to be pithy, playful, yet deadly serious about bringing theology to the masses. The more I thought about the mission of Fortress and their Theology for the People initiative, the more excited I was about being able to contribute.

Still, the challenge of writing a book without theory, method, jargon, or any of those other academic tools/crutches was more daunting than I anticipated. Striking that balance between engaging and informative can be a clumsy dance and many toes can be stepped on by the time it's over. I hope you read something in here that's food for the journey and you can benefit from my mistakes. I made the deliberate choice in dealing with the end times to concentrate on the particular strand of theology that currently holds so much cultural power over our imagination—dispensationalism and Rapture culture. If you don't know what those words mean, then this book's for you. If you do know what those words mean, then this book's still for you, as I break down the biblical, historical, and theological foundations upon which this theological hot mess rests.

As always, a community of people stand behind any book, and I want to thank Tripp Fuller and Tony Jones for their trust in letting me contribute a volume to this series. Tony especially deserves deep gratitude for his suggestions and patience at those times when I didn't take them. The folks at Fortress have been amazing to work with and I am fortunate to have such a fine community guide me through another book. I'm deeply appreciative of my colleagues in the Religious Studies Department at Elon University. L. D. Russell, Brian Pennington, Amy Allocco, Ariela Marcus-Sells, Toddie Peters, and Pamela Winfield have been wonderful conversation partners over the years. Lynn Huber and Geoffrey Claussen, however, deserve special thanks. Professor Claussen read over parts of this manuscript and offered helpful suggestions to keep me from mistakes I would have regretted. Professor Huber was extremely generous with her library and is one of the most insightful and intriguing scholars working on apocalyptic literature today. I have grown enormously because of all these fine people.

I am also grateful for the presence of Jan Rivero in my life. She not only supports the solitary work of a writer, but serves as an astute theological partner who keeps me honest and grounded with the concerns of her parish. Her most important challenge is to continually question whose needs does theology serve? I think that is the same question Fortress asks with their new publishing initiative. So, have fun and keep watching.

Easter, 2016

The Dread of Endings

Who cannot see that the world is already in its decline, and no longer has the strength and vigor of former times? There is no need to invoke Scripture authority to prove it. The world tells its own tale and in its general decadence bears adequate witness that it is approaching the end. . . . There is less innocence in the courts, less justice in the judges, less concord between friends, less artistic sincerity, less moral strictness.

Cyprian, 250 CE

If you're ever bored and want to see what an alternative universe looks like, spend some time at www.rapture ready.com. Go ahead, do it now; I'll wait. Back? Great. How was that for a WTF moment? Perhaps you spent the first five minutes thinking to yourself, "This is one of the most amazing pieces of performance art I've ever seen, rivaling Banksey's Bemusement Park, #Dismaland." But then as you scrolled through the site you realized, "Holy

1

Crap! These people really believe this, and we let them vote, drive cars, and procreate." Perhaps you were stunned

THE BISHOP

As a Mainline Protestant I'm pretty sure the Rapture Ready website is NSFW.

to find that on the "Rapture Index" we're close to the all-time high of 188 points. Jesus is calling, but not so tenderly this time. Welcome to the amazing world of Raptureland, a glance through the looking glass of those who obsess about the end times.

Apocalypse. Armageddon. The Eschaton. Springing from our fascination with The End, a storehouse of images permeates our art, literature, and religion. The End is a belief so ingrained within us that the apocalypse is part of the air we breathe, the atmosphere that envelops us. Themes about the end of the world as we know it, to borrow from REM, saturate our consciousness because they're so pervasive. The film industry would probably go broke if it didn't have the idea of The End to mine for material. Of course, perhaps after the movie *This Is The End*, #thismoviesucks, Hollywood deserves to go bankrupt, or at the very least we should have an actor-shaming tumblr featuring James Franco, Seth Rogen, and the rest of those cynical money-grubbers who showed up in this hot mess. (Hermione, what were you thinking?) Apocalyptic themes run through every culture, every religion, from ancient times to our own.

Humankind's dirty little secret is that The End fascinates us.

The word *apocalypse* doesn't denote the end of all things, rather it means to uncover or unveil something that is hidden. In apocalyptic literature the curtain is pulled back from the façade of existence so that we can see the reality behind the scenes. It's like the moment in the *Wizard of Oz* when the curtain is pulled back to reveal the truth about the great and powerful Oz—he's just a guy who uses technology to create an illusion of power. Ancient apocalypses from Babylon to Israel worked to show that behind the scenes of everyday life, with its oppressions and violence, God's reality was far different. These writings revealed that the forces behind the scrim, evil or divine, were a reflection of another, heavenly, reality. This revelation was often ambiguous because when the apocalyptic truth was revealed, confusion entered the picture. An unveiling of evil spiritual forces for some was for others the very system that keeps the world orderly. Revelation of what God thought about society—and God was seldom pleased—called one's very existence into question.

Meeting the Apocalypse for the First Time

My first exposure to the contemporary world of Christian apocalyptic speculation came in 1972 when I was a sophomore in college. It was right after a profoundly compelling conversionary moment in my life. At the time I considered it a unique and singular event, but I have since come to understand life as a series of conversionary moments. A nineteen-year-old, however, doesn't often possess the means to adequately interpret experience, which made me a perfect target for those who embraced my fledgling faith and proceeded to put a copy of Hal Lindsey's *The Late Great Planet Earth* into my hands. Little did I know I was getting ready to take Mr. Hal's wild, apocalyptic ride. Giving me that book was like putting matches in a baby's crib—not good for the baby or the crib.

THE ACOLYTE

I think it would be hard to take a preacher named Hal seriously.

I absorbed Lindsey's pithy and clever interpretations of biblical prophecy with a morbid and naïve curiosity. I felt as if I were in possession of the secret code to understand a world that was falling apart. How had no one ever told me about this before? Lindsey even had maps of how the armies of the Earth would converge on Israel for the last battle, *maps* for God's sake! How much clearer could it all be? When I asked my new friends why this stuff wasn't taught in the churches, I was informed the church was part of the problem, but we in the know had information that most churches didn't possess; it was all part of their apostasy that they wouldn't believe us. For a teenager, having the roadmap to the end of the world was like taking acid, but without all the painful headaches and legal complications. The landmarks were the same, but totally skewed and colorfully messy, with a soupçon of fear and paranoia thrown in for good measure. I had fallen down the rabbit hole and I couldn't get back.

So many things make
more sense with a chart!
And Daniel 7 references!

THE DEACON

Over the course of a few days I absorbed Lindsey's
mesmerizing tale of worldwide calamity. It was a won-
drous story. The countdown to Jesus' return and the end
of the world began with the return of Jews to Israel in
1948. Since then the clock has been ticking, and at any
moment millions of people will suddenly disappear from
the face of the earth. A perplexed and sinful world will
be stunned by this event, but, unfortunately for them,
they have seven years of horrific tribulation left before
the last great battle, Armageddon. During this seven-year
period a charismatic charmer will emerge who will lead
the world and help Israel rebuild its temple. But unlike
all those other sociopaths, #politicians, who manipulate
us with charm and personality, this one will be the Antichrist. Solidifying his power through a ten-nation con-
federation, probably the European Common Market (this
was 1972 after all), the Antichrist will come to dominate
most of the political orders of the earth. At the middle of
the seven years the Antichrist puts his image in the rebuilt
Temple of Jerusalem, at which point events accelerate to
the final battle, Armageddon, in the valley of Megiddo in
Israel. This is the moment Jesus returns with the saints
to really kick some pagan ass. My adolescent brain was
fascinated by the graphics in tracts and pop Christian culture back then—lurid images of ascending bodies leaving crashing cars, plummeting planes, and empty graves.

Zombies for Jesus. It was electrifying to think I was living in the last days.

I was so captivated by Hal Lindsey's interpretations of the world that I dropped out of the godless world of secular education (though, in fairness, bad lifestyle choices had been leading to this moment). When you can pin skipping class and dropping out of college on following Jesus it makes it all seem more holy somehow. Leaving behind my former life, I embarked on my East Coast Armageddon Hitchhiking tour, earnestly warning all those I met of the wrath to come. It was, of course, the early seventies, so I wasn't the only one taken with the story of impending apocalypse. *The Late Great Planet Earth* was the best-selling nonfiction book in the 1970s, a success that only continued, selling more than 28 million copies by 1990. This should give us pause: there are millions of decent, God-fearing folk who sincerely believe that Hal Lindsey actually knows what he's talking about.

In the course of my travels I encountered a group who would super-size my apocalyptic imagination—the Children of God. Hal Lindsey, I soon realized, was a timid poser who would only commit to an outer edge of 1988 for the return of Christ. The Children of God, a.k.a., Family of Love, a.k.a., the Family, were ready to commit to a more immediate time frame, and in order to flee God's judgment we were told that we had to leave the United States before the elections of 1972. Boy, was I lucky to have run into them! Just in the nick of time! They knew the Bible better than Hal Lindsey, and their story seemed even more compelling. We were the vanguard of new prophets warning a corrupt and decadent age that The End was near. It was all very dramatic, though that wooden yoke (Jeremiah

27:2) they made us wear around our necks when we went out to do street theater was a bit cumbersome.

These types of stories are scary. Funny. But scary.

THE ELDER

Four disillusioned months after entering the Children of God I found myself in a rowhouse in Toronto, Ontario looking at a roomful of my new best friends and wondering how I had been so deceived, so foolish, as to fall for this delusional tale of doom. Slipping away from them like a thief in the night, I headed to the Love Inn, a farm outside of Ithaca in upstate New York. One of the many alternative Christian communities that sprouted like mushrooms during the Jesus Movement of the sixties and seventies, this community took me in, put me to work, and eventually my apocalyptic fever dreams faded as I came to understand that I had fallen into the peculiar world of Rapture culture.[1]

Rapture Culture

Who doesn't love a good disaster story (how else to explain the box office for the horribly titled movie, *Armageddon*?), and what could be more disastrous than the end of the world? It's hard to resist the seductive allure of thinking that our time is special, that we live in the most important period of history and it all ends with us. This belief has fueled a powerhouse industry of books, movies, speakers, and churches that have influenced millions of people around the world by use of fiction, conferences, and media appearances. Call it The Left Behind Industrial Complex.

THE DEACON

You got out early. Just imagine a youth group trip to the theater to pay our friends to watch Kurt Cameron in *Left Behind*. *#EyesClosedHeadBowedDuringCredits*

According to recent polls, ten to fifteen million Americans are doctrinal believers in the end times, and another ten to fifteen million are "narrative" believers, accepting the rough outlines of what we shall see is the dispensational interpretation. A Time/CNN poll taken in the aftermath of 9/11 found that 59 percent of Americans believed the events in Revelation are going to come true in their lifetimes.

The world of the apocalypse still exercises an enormous influence on a significant part of the Christian community in America and beyond. A teenager, caught in the liminal stages of life, can be excused many indiscretions, but we all know many people who sincerely believe that Jesus could come back any minute. In a recent poll, 41 percent of all U.S. adults, 54 percent of Protestants, and 77 percent of evangelicals believe that the world is living in the biblical end times.[2] It might be easy to dismiss this study because it was commissioned for the release of a book on the end times, but a recent poll by the Public Religion Research Institute mirrored these numbers, showing that 77 percent of white evangelical Protestants believed climate change is happening because we're living in the last days.[3]

This sounds judgmental because it is. How do these people get to vote or hold office?

THE ELDER

It's hard to find a person, at least in American culture, who has not heard of the *Left Behind* books. The website www.LeftBehind.com claims over 69 million readers of at least one of the books in their series. Millions more saw the movie, *Left Behind*, where multitudes disappeared, along with Nicholas Cage's career, in the blink of an eye. Millions are convinced, as I once was, that the Rapture is a thing that could be upon us at any moment and we will then, in the words of the late Christian songwriter/singer

---

The third time I got saved was at a middle school youth camp to DC Talk's cover of Larry Norman.

THE DEACON

Larry Norman's most famous hit, "Wish We'd All Been Ready." The anticipated return of Christ is so clearly evident to those who live in this community, have internalized its narrative, and immersed themselves in books, movies, podcasts, and conferences, that to try and break through the interpretive world they've constructed is futile. When I question these beliefs in the Rapture and Jesus' return I'm met with the same shake of head I used to give those who tried to convince me that my convictions were misplaced.

The attraction of Christ's return is so strong because we're shaped by stories, and as stories go, this one has staying power. It's become a commonplace idea that narratives shape us, constructing the mental landscape we move through. Those narratives we choose to embrace and take into our daily lives become something more than mere stories; they are the living room furniture of the spaces we inhabit, and some days it's hard to get off the couch. This is especially true when we feel beaten down by life. If we feel besieged by a culture that doesn't respect our values and we're powerless to affect the decisions the elites make about our lives, we resonate with stories that offer us certainty that God is in control. Perhaps we harbor hope that we will be vindicated at The End, when all things are revealed for what they truly were behind the screen. This day of reversal is part of God's ultimate plan, and if we only hang on long enough everyone will know we were right.

To be part of a cosmic story is to be placed at the center of existence. There's a strong appeal to a life of meaning when life seems meaningless. The Rapture narrative

and all that accompanies it offers us a story we can participate in. When anything of significance happens in Israel,
it's not just business as usual in the Mideast; it's the fulfillment of biblical prophecy. With every headline about
ISIS beheading another Christian, or the possibility of
Iran acquiring nuclear weapons, we become susceptible
to a story that explains that the world is not spinning out
of control, but heading irrevocably toward The End and
everything is happening just as God intends. Ours is not
the only generation that has thought so; millions of people
over thousands of years have interpreted world events in
relation to the end times drama.[4]

The pull of The End is so strong that it affects secular
pursuits as well. Themes that are prominent in Jewish and
Christian apocalypses—alienation/salvation/eternal life/
heaven/hell—even drive the world of modern technology
and science fiction. The inventor Ray Kurzweil, for example, author of the influential book *The Singularity Is Near*,
probes how far he can extend human life by downloading
our consciousness into a computer, perhaps keeping us alive
until we're able to merge with the energy of the universe.
Not exactly the type of life everlasting that the Revelation
of John addresses, but the idea is there. The apocalyptic
imagination created by Jewish and Christian texts, with
their dualist worldview, desire to overcome human suffering, and hope for resurrected human bodies finds expression in the world of Silicon Valley (#Robert Geraci,
#ApocalypticAI). The world of virtual reality, of Second
Life, is a counterpart to heaven, where lives are not lost, but
continue on without end. As long as cyberspace exists we can
live forever and create a world without the flaws of this one.

The desire to live forever is the only reason I can think of for the *Highlander* movies. There is even an entire movement, transhumanism, exploring ways in which we can transcend the human body to enhance ourselves for everlasting life.

THE BISHOP

I don't know which is weirder to me— raptured to heaven or a second online life.

Hope for happy endings is a very powerful category for shaping our consciousness. Apocalyptic categories deeply influence those who are working in artificial intelligence and related fields, though they may not be aware of this fact. If, as religious traditions tell us, we're oppressed by the fragility of our humanity, then the downloading of our consciousness into machines constitutes a resurrection of sorts. Transcendence comes in our ability to overcome bodily limitations. These themes are growing increasingly common in science fiction, which explores through books, movies, and television the destruction and salvation that artificial intelligence promises (#*Transcendence, #JohnnyDepp*). In transhumanism we find concepts that are ancient and resistant to abolition. In the world of techno-salvation the heavenly city of Revelation has been replaced with cyberspace, a place of re-enchantment where lives can be created that will live forever.

Sensational Dispensationalism

The influence of apocalyptic imagination may be subtler outside of religious traditions, but within religious communities the idea that we know the future, that biblical prophecy foretells what is to come, attracts millions to embrace dispensationalist theology. The term *dispensationalism* refers to an innovative path of biblical interpretation that started in nineteenth-century England among the Plymouth Brethren and has shaped American Christianity in significant ways. Dispensational theology alludes to distinct periods of time, dispensations, in which God purportedly deals in different ways with the world. Adam and Eve lived in one dispensation, Noah in another, Moses in another, and so on. In each of these eras, the work of God to bring judgment and salvation was different. All those who have accepted the dispensationalist interpretation believe that it's probable we're living in the last dispensation or era of God's time and that the Rapture, the taking of believing Christians from this world, is an imminent event that could occur at any moment. For them, the Bible is a blueprint of the future, revealing God's plan for planet Earth. This feeds into our desire to know what the future holds. Given the abundance of examples of divination and astrology in antiquity, this fascination with the future has been present in humankind for a long time. Is it the case, however, that the Bible is a roadmap into our future? A closer look at how scriptural prophecy functions offers us other lenses with which to "read" our world.

When we contemplate our future we may find ourselves caught between optimism and pessimism. One of

THE BISHOP

I have never thought the Bible mapped out the end, but I am constantly struck with how many in our churches believe this.

the reasons that the *Left Behind* phenomenon exercises such cultural power is that a clear cold look at the world shows us that human behavior doesn't engender much confidence in our ability to manage our affairs. We may be more technologically adept and sophisticated, but we use this knowledge to create ingenious ways to destroy ourselves. Jesus' imminent return offers believers a reason for optimism in the face of our propensity for destruction. The *Left Behind* narrative feeds into a certain way of comprehending the world that matches up with the realities we see around us. If things are unsettled in the Middle East, the believer knows it's all according to God's plan, not the schemes of the political architects of the Project for the New American Century (Google it). The dispensational scenario knits the fragments of life into a meaningful whole and the Rapture becomes a social rhetoric that places us in the great cosmic drama. If we want to know where we fit in the plan, we can turn to the Rapture preachers or prophecy books to tell us.

If you live in America, dispensationalists will even show how America's role is also prophesied in the Bible (though the more honest ones will hedge their bets considerably about this). It's not just America they find in the

I went to a Youth For Christ event once. Their nationalism freaked me out more than their Jesus-is-my-boyfriend songs. Ohh the fog machine was a bit much.

THE ACOLYTE

Bible, other nations not even in existence when the Bible was written play a role in their interpretation of ancient prophecies. Whether it's the common interpretation of communist Russia as Gog in the book of Ezekiel, Lindsey's offensive description of China as "The Yellow Peril," or the present fear of all things Islam in many contemporary interpreters like Tim LaHaye or John Hagee; all threats to the American way of life, democracy, and even the "free" market, according to the dispensationalists, are found in biblical writings recorded thousands of years ago.

This distinctive form of Christian faith understands itself in relation to its enemies in modernity as an embattled church seeking to stem the tide of unbelief in a faithless culture. Dispensationalists have been quick to identify the forces of the Antichrist with anyone who threatened the American way of life. Sometimes this was the Bolshevik, other times the Feminist, but always it was anyone who called the status quo into question. One result of this thinking means that there have been many antichrists over the last 150 years. My grandmother told me she thought Franklin Delano Roosevelt was the Antichrist, but I was sure she was mistaken about this because the

Antichrist would never have given us the Blue Ridge Parkway. Of course, in the theological logic of those who believe we're in the last days, the devil will give us the desires of our hearts in order to ensnare us. If the Antichrist will give Israel the third Temple of Jerusalem at the end of time, the Blue Ridge Parkway is like an appetizer of temptation to worship the forces of socialism.

THE ELDER

I had to hide my Grandmother's posts on Facebook after she identified the Anti-Christ in the WHITE house in 2008.

In fairness, secularists also have their apocalyptic candidates for satanic control of the world: predatory capitalism and the ever-increasing panopticon of national security and absolute state power. The temptation to Manichaeism is no respecter of political positions, but this is what the apocalyptic mindset does: it populates the world with current actors who reflect a strong dualism of good and evil. Who stands on the various sides of that divide is usually determined by the social location of whoever is writing, creating, or interpreting apocalyptic literature. We have only to read through the prophecy genre unleashed by Hal Lindsey and others to find a projection of our current fears. While communist Russia was at the center of Lindsey's interpretation, secular humanists and Muslims show up as villains in contemporary prophecy fiction.

Ample work has been done on showing how ideas of Christ's return reflect the ideologies of our cultural fears and contemporary villains, but behind our views of the end times are also theological assumptions about God and God's interaction with the world. Those inclined to dispensationalist views see God as the omniscient, transcendent, omnipotent ruler who breaks into history at certain crucial moments to move the chess pieces around the board. In the apocalyptic version of this story found in the book of Revelation, God returns as a warrior ready to slaughter God's enemies for their persecution of the saints. A select few will escape planetary disaster, but for the rest, there will be enormous suffering. It is often unnerving to see how those who believe they will be raptured welcome this coming destruction of their enemies.

I find it odd that Christians can insist God desires destruction for the same enemies Jesus insists we love and prayer for.

THE BISHOP

Imagining the Apocalypse

If you're still reeling from your visit to www.raptureready .com take heart, this is only one small segment of Christianity's understanding of The End. Since Jesus' first appearance, the church has conceived of ways in which Christ returns that are more nuanced and hopeful. Yes, we developed a number of strange terms about it—"Are you a dispensational premillennialist?" "No, I'm an amillennialist, realized eschatology kind of guy. How dare you call me a premillennialist!"—but the images, metaphors, and narratives we confront in the apocalypses of sacred texts offer fascinating diversity. Interpretation is like that, and as much as it pains me to say it, dispensationalists are part of the family. Sure, they may remind us of weird uncle Tommy sitting in the corner at family gatherings crookedly grinning at the rest of us as we try to figure out whether to be amused or terrified, but they're still part of our story.

Many Christians understand the heart of this story as God immersing God's very self within a world coming to be. The Incarnation is the center of Christian hope. In this profound image of embodiment, God doesn't escape the pain and suffering of the world, but experiences it in the most intimate way in order to draw the world into the divine life. As people of the Incarnation, we should not welcome the Rapture loophole or desire to escape in order to gloat or revel in the suffering of others. As we shall see later, the return of Christ has also meant the hard work of being God's body, bringing healing to the world so that the good creation of God might flourish. The Rapture as an escape hatch from suffering contradicts the very heart of Christian faith.

THE ACOLYTE

I hope so. I have to admit I was a bit skittish up to this point.

A variety of theological perspectives about The End have been present in Christianity from the beginning, most notably from its roots in Judaism. Inasmuch as these perspectives reflect the cultural worlds they come from, Christian tradition manifests certain ideas and theologies that shape all those who have been introduced to them. How we discern the will of God within these transitory, historical moments influences how we live, raise our children, and vote. Theologies, like ideas, have consequences and ideas about The End have had enormous influence on American society, often in ways we don't recognize. Take the poll mentioned earlier about climate change. If you believe that drought or flood caused by human exploitation of the earth is merely a part of the way things are going to be in the last days, you have no motivation whatsoever to do anything to change the situation; no need to pay attention to Pope Francis's encyclical, *Laudato Si*. If we degrade the resources of the planet it's all simply according to God's plan.

I see a two-fold challenge today. One, we help people move beyond the Rapture

THE BISHOP

ready ideology. Two, we pass on a faith without such a twisted ideology at its center.

The apocalyptic imagination motivates millions, coding the world for them and narrating ways that God may or may not be present. If you live in the mental world of Babylon needing to be destroyed and study the Rapture Index daily, you may be inclined to hunker down and wait for God's judgment on a filth-filled world. If you believe that this world is the good creation of God, and we have a responsibility to manifest the grace of God in it, to make known the new heaven in the new earth, your life looks quite different. At the risk of dualistic simplicity, how we internalize our understanding of God determines how we engage with the world.

Faith can lead us to withdraw from the world as a place so fallen, so hopelessly godless, that we should not be "yoked" with unbelievers (2 Corinthians 6:14), and should "come out from among them" (6:17). Those of you reading this book probably don't think this way, but it's very possible you have friends who do. Withdrawal has always been one way that some Christians, mostly fundamentalists, have responded to the challenges of the world around them. A conviction of Christ's imminent return shapes how you view the institutions and ethos of surrounding culture.

I was reminded of this at a gathering I attended in Seoul, South Korea when the woman beside me started up a conversation. It was obvious that she was a fundamentalist, so trying to keep matters light, I talked about my children and the wonderful public school they were in. As I talked her face scrunched up, lips disappearing into her mouth, and her eyes took on a feral glow. "You should take your children out of that pagan, secular humanist school. They'll lose their faith." It never crossed my mind that I was glimpsing the future war against American public education in that encounter.

Withdrawal is not the only response of those who accept the dispensational perspective, especially as it concerns Israel. Millions of Christians believe that the final war will be fought over Israel and that absolute and unequivocal support for Israel and anything it does is a mark of faith. Those who embrace "Christian Zionism" are doing much to shape American foreign policy and they exercise considerable influence in Congress. It was not widely known that Ronald Reagan had an absolute fascination with evangelical apocalypticism. He discussed *The Late Great Planet Earth* with many of his friends and once told a California state senator, "For the first time ever, everything is in place for the battle of Armageddon and the second coming of Christ."[5] He mentioned to others that his generation might be the one that saw Armageddon and even after winning the White House, he made repeated references to the end of days. I wonder if he ever had these conversations with Nancy's astrologer.

More recently, George W. Bush revealed his apocalyptic mindset when he divided up the world into the righteous and the evildoers in a speech at West Point in 2002. While Bush may not have shared the depth of premillennial convictions his evangelical base did, the neoconservative idea of remaking the Middle East did connect with evangelical apocalypticism. According to some accounts, Bush invoked Ezekiel's prophecy to French President Jacques Chirac to justify the invasion of Iraq. "'Gog and Magog are at work in the Middle East,' the American president apparently explained. 'Biblical prophecies are being fulfilled.' 'This confrontation,' he continued, 'is willed by God, who wants to use this conflict to erase His people's enemies before a new age begins.'"[6]

I'll have more to say about the connection between American evangelicalism and Israel later, but it should shock us that Hal Lindsey did consulting work on global politics for both the Pentagon and the Israeli government.[7] That's like asking Donald Trump for advice on how to treat Narcissistic Personality Disorder.

THE DEACON

I just spit my coffee on this book. That would be a HUGE mistake.

Most of us realize that our beliefs have material effects in the world, and because of this it's vital to reflect critically on those consequences. This is often difficult for us because we're so embedded within the world our ideas have constructed that we don't even take time to think about where our beliefs come from. The historical journey of an idea, or even a theology, from its inception to the place where we've internalized it and believe it to be a truth always held, can be circuitous and hidden from us.

As a thought experiment, think of the way our world would look if the book of Revelation had never made it into the Bible. There was great debate in the early church about whether to even allow the book into the New Testament, and it was the last one the church accepted. Even so, it's had a mixed reception among Christians. When we consider how different the world of art and literature, of politics and culture might look without the storehouse of images from Revelation, the entire idea of the second coming might have been something we consigned to those who lived during the time of Jesus. Without Revelation (not to mention the other assorted biblical texts used to construct dispensationalism) as a guiding authority for the beliefs of millions in history, the world would look, and possibly feel, very different from the one we live in.

We should all be interested in how biblical writings and the history of interpretation impact our contemporary life. Beliefs create images of God that we put great faith and hope in. Ideas such as the Rapture are the products of human ingenuity that create enormous expectation. The Bible is a powerful authority for Christian faith and practice, but we often invest a particular interpretation of the Bible with the authority of the text itself, putting us in a defensive position if the interpretation is questioned.

For those who have constructed their world around the belief that we're in the last days, whose very identity is shaped by the urgency of living at the end of time, my questions about how to interpret the book of Revelation is proof of prophecy coming true: "First of all you must understand this, that in the last days scoffers will come, scoffing and indulging their own lusts and saying, 'Where is the promise of his coming? For ever since our ancestors died, all things continue as they were from the beginning of creation'" (2 Peter 3:3–4). A rigorous examination of ideas, however, is not necessarily scoffing at those who believe in the imminent return of Christ; I've also known what it's like to embrace these ideas, and to shape my world around them.

Christian reflection on these themes has been labeled *eschatology*, which comes from the Greek *eschaton*, indicating the last things. Eschatology is about God acting in and through history, and in this sense the notion of old ages passing away and new ages taking their place is a recurring theme in the Bible. According to scripture, both Jesus and his followers believed that the new age was upon them, but this new age was also a view widely shared by others who were writing Jewish eschatological texts at that time. Expectation is a part of apocalyptic texts; often taking the form of hope that oppression will cease.

This expectation of relief from oppression, and vindication when God's justice comes, is a recurring theme in Jewish and Christian apocalyptic texts. In fact, there is a legitimate question about whether there is even such a thing as Christian eschatology, or whether it's all Jewish, including the book of Revelation. Apocalypses are not so concerned about the details of the end of the world, but the responsibilities of those who seek to be faithful to God in the midst of oppression. Heaven is not as important as the deliverance that the Son of Man—a figure of no small speculation over the centuries—brings. The books of Daniel and Revelation don't envision roadmaps of the future, but hope in the midst of oppression. In the midst of enormous suffering the message was, God delivers. It's like Domino's Pizza, but different because God takes a little more time.

Living in the shadow of the Roman Empire, the early church manifested an alternative way of living in the world that called into question the order that empire always labors to establish—the ability to dictate the terms of what the "real world" looks like. This refusal to accept the empire's vision sparked apathy and rage both before and after Jesus lived. The way some of us read apocalyptic literature today would have been incomprehensible to the communities for which it was originally written. The compelling message of liberation has been eroded into fodder for the apocalyptic fever dreams of those who desire to escape the world more than they hope for God's grace to be made manifest in it.

To avoid the crazies I think I've just avoided the apocalyptic literature all together.

THE ELDER

There are multitudes of other ways of interpreting the biblical texts that might allow us to shape the world toward something other than Armageddon. A theology that wants to see the earth destroyed and quietly harbors the self-righteous desire to prove to others that it's right and all the rest are wrong leads to a far different place than a theology that sees the world as the good creation of God, gifted with the exquisite beauty of the mundane, where the life of God is known in small but powerful ways.

We wait, as generations before us have waited. The question is *how* do we wait? Living between the already and not yet, struggling with suffering, even evil, we find ourselves wondering when is the hope of his coming? A large part of the answer to that question is found in what precisely it is that we wait for. If we're waiting for the rider on the white horse to vanquish our enemies, show them the truth, while riding through rivers of their blood, that expectation leads us into certain behaviors that ensure we'll get what we want. If, however, our patient waiting is for the Lamb of God, who gives his life in love, then we have another path to follow. Let's take a closer look at how those paths were forged.

2

Apocalypse Then

Other spectacles remain, as well: that last unending day of judgment; that day unlooked for by the nations, regarded by them with derision, when the world, hoary with age, and all that it has produced, shall be consumed in one great flame! How vast a spectacle then will burst upon the eye!

Tertullian, *Spectacles*, 197–202 CE

What if I told you that everything you've believed for the last four months is a lie?"

"Morpheus?"

"No, dude, not Morpheus; he won't show up for another twenty-seven years."

"Oh, well shut up Satan."

"No, not Satan either; it's just your freaking reason trying to break through all the bamboozlement."

"They said that would happen."

"What would happen?"

"That I might get tempted to doubt what they taught me."

"That's because they're teaching you bs. Seriously, just think about it for a minute. Look around you. Are you happy having brown sugar and maple instant oatmeal every day? Enjoying the bulgur slop you get for lunch? How are those day-old Dunkin' Donuts working out for you? Why are we even having this conversation?"

"They've been right about the earthquakes and floods, the social unrest and political upheaval. We elected Nixon president for God's sake."

"So? There are earthquakes and floods all the time. This is nothing new. Everything that they're telling you is so unique to your time is just the same as it's always been. And, sorry to say, there's going to be more earthquakes, floods, and wars. As for Nixon, well, you ain't seen nothing yet."

"God, you're annoying."

"I'm pissing you off because you're starting to realize that whatever this is, is stupid."

"But . . . they sound like they know what they're talking about. Besides, I needed a place to park myself for a while; I'm in a liminal stage."

"Stop whining, it's unattractive. They sound authoritative because they memorized a script you've never heard before, gave it their spin, and now exist in a world they created."

"Don't we all?"

"Point taken, but this is different. Their imaginations have stopped and they're caught in a feedback loop they can't escape from. Right now, we've gotta get out of this place, if it's the last thing we ever do."

"Will there be a better life for me and you?"

"I'm not making any promises on that one given your decision-making skills, but start making your escape plans and we'll take it from there."

Though on any given day there are a multitude of voices in my head having conversations, when I was in the Children of God I managed to listen to the right one. But as I was to learn, their spiel fit a pattern. See if this sounds familiar: A time is soon coming when tribulation and calamity will plague the earth in natural disasters, especially earthquakes and floods, creating great havoc among all the people on the planet. In this moment of tribulation there will be enormous political and social upheaval and multitudes will suffer. Eventually there will be a great battle against Israel and those who war against the saints will be overcome and destroyed; then comes a judgment of the unrighteous by the Messiah, at which time God will deal decisively with the Gentiles. At the end of the old age the new age will commence and the righteous dead will enjoy eternal life.[1]

In high school, my family's church had a weekend seminar on preparing for Y2K.  **THE DEACON** Army surplus shopping for Jesus!

If you thought you'd heard that story before, you're not alone. All these themes are found in numerous apocalyptic texts, both biblical and nonbiblical, written from the early second or late third century BCE to the first century CE. Apocalypses were important stories, not just to Jews, but to all those who lived in antiquity. Apocalyptic tales formed part of what philosopher Charles Taylor calls the "social imaginary," a set of ideas that shape and form society.[2] The biblical writers knew these stories, the expectations and hopes found in them; even the fears that would've been shaped by them. What might help us today is to realize how much these stories shape us as well.

Prediction or Comfort?

What I didn't know at the time of my first exposure to Rapture culture is that Jewish apocalyptic literature, the source of Christian speculation about the last days, drew from its own traditions and origins. Books like I Enoch, which contained numerous apocalyptic texts, borrowed from surrounding cultures to construct texts that served certain polemical ends. The book of Daniel used ideas like the "Son of Man" from those earlier writings, but gave those concepts its own spin. In these ancient writings we find common elements that might sound familiar to us: the division of history into the old and new age; a stark battle between good and evil; the determination of the future by God; extensive use of symbol and metaphor; dreams, visions, or a journey to the heavenly realm so the writer could see what was "really" going on behind the scenes; numerology; an expectation of the end; and God's final judgment so that injustice not prevail. Jewish writings drew upon Persian, Babylonian, and Hellenist ideas, such as the periodization of history. It's no surprise that the dispensationalists continue this tradition.

When we encounter apocalyptic images and stories in the biblical texts we're not discovering anything new or novel. Before Jesus spoke of the destruction of the temple, Daniel wrote of four kingdoms, or John described his vision of great beasts with ten horns, there were others who had laid the groundwork for these images. The path

---

I like to think of apocalyptic literature like science fiction: an amazing genre that's **THE DEACON** straight up crazy if you take it literally.

---

from biblical and nonbiblical texts concerning the struggle of good and evil to Armageddon is a complex one, keeping scholars busy for centuries, but for us the point is that as we think about the end times, we're not doing so in a vacuum. Large amounts of literature exist that are antecedents to the ideas in the Bible.

We simply cannot take the Bible, lift it out of its various contexts, and ignore the influences that contributed to its production over time. That would be like taking the Pope out of Rome, Queen Elizabeth out of England, the Dalai Lama out of Tibet . . . oh, wait. Well, you get the point, right? You have to look at the big picture. When we consider all the choices before us, we can feel overwhelmed. Are apocalyptic texts like Daniel or Revelation predictions of the future, or do they address the times in which they were written, reflecting ideas that were well known to their readers? How we answer this question takes us a long way to deciding how we'll understand books like Daniel or Revelation, or even Jesus and Paul.

For some people, the apocalyptic passages of the Bible must be read as an unfolding of future events known only to God who revealed them to the writers. Other readers find things far more profound in biblical texts than mere prediction. They discover in these writings something richer—hope in the midst of difficult circumstances, or a call to faithfulness when the necessity to confront the orders we have constructed turn against us and run on their own demonic energy. I know, this isn't as sexy as knowing the future and then convincing people you know something they don't, but it may be better for the soul in the long run.

It's not as if the ancient world didn't believe in pre-diction, but I'm suggesting that prediction is a thin way to understand texts rich in metaphorical images meant to evoke in readers ideas about God and the ways in which God works in the world. For those who are taken with the *Left Behind* books, who have embraced the innovative interpretations that those books are based on, my sugges-tion that mere prediction is a flattening out of the rich tex-ture of the biblical apocalypses will seem like heresy (not that there's anything wrong with that).

The Way We Were Is the Way We Are

We accept certain ideas about God and the world because of the authority we give the sources of those beliefs. The Bible, tradition, reason, and experience—all these function as authorities for us in diverse ways. Dispensationalism requires an inerrant Bible and a literal reading to main-tain its system. Inerrancy is the belief that the Bible is God's word and without error in any matter (geography, history, cosmology, etc.). Every word in the King James Bible (because obviously this is the way that Jesus spoke it and Paul wrote it) can be trusted absolutely as the revela-tion of God. Every single word of the Bible has equal authority because it's perfect information from God (though let's face it, there's not a lot of consistency here, given our desire to keep our eyes and hands, Matthew 5:27–30). This approach allows those like Hal Lindsey or Tim LaHaye, and all the rest who work that territory, to

---

How is this the same
religion I'm in?

THE ELDER

---

pull scriptures from different places and use them to con-struct the narrative that fits their perspective. If every pas-sage has equal weight, it's easy to stitch pieces together to create what you want. Think of it like putting together a jigsaw puzzle, but from Salvador Dali. Everything's in there; it just looks . . . strange. ("Daddy, why is that arm hanging from the tree? OMG!!! The tree has eyes! I hate museums daddy; why did you bring me here?)

Because of their belief in the inerrancy of the Bible, many dispensationalists refuse to consider that truth comes to us in a variety of ways. If we accept the literal path as the only way toward truth, we're shut off from a rich world of understanding, a world of textures that can only be known and felt through story and metaphor. This is a point that Frederick Buechner makes so profoundly in his book *Telling the Truth: The Gospel as Tragedy, Comedy, and Fairy Tale*. He shows how the gospel itself is a kind of fairy tale, where rough beasts are saved by beauty's kiss and those who are blinded finally see. You could think of apocalyptic stories in the same way. Some stories are so amazing that a literal reading erases their power to narrate another world for us, a world of possibilities where no one is beyond redemption.

One temptation of dispensational interpretation is to pull the text too quickly into our age, arguing that the meaning was unknown until now. This only serves to domesticate both the text and God. When we say that

---

THE BISHOP

The domestication of scripture takes many forms. Some of us use robes, stoles, and sermons under 12 minutes.

---

events in our age constitute the true meaning of the Bible and that history can only happen in just such a way, we're demanding a God in a box (like Jack in a Box, but when God pops out of the dispensationalist's box it's much, much, scarier). Since dispensationalists believe their interpretations are true, God can only act according to those readings. Any other interpretation about God's action in the world is wrong.

This brings us to a crucial consideration: How *do* we read apocalyptic texts in our time? If apocalyptic writings have a rich historical background and draw from diverse ancient sources to paint their poetic and sometimes horrifying pictures, shouldn't we just relegate them to the past and not bother trying to interpret them for our age? It's all so obscure anyway and ancient writings have nothing to do with us today. I mean, there's no mention of Kendrick Lamar, Taylor Swift, or Star Wars, so how important can all that old stuff be anyway?

Here's the thing though—we live narrated lives and are still being shaped by ancient stories, often in ways we're unaware of. As in any story, there are always fresh insights available to us. We read scripture because it helps us understand ourselves and our relationship with God. Originally written for other audiences, we struggle to relate to apocalypses. The writers of the biblical texts were struggling with things difficult for us to relate to and understand. Our distance from the ancient world means it's hard to know exactly how the texts were heard originally:

"What was that?"

"I don't know. . . ."

"I think it was 'Blessed are the cheese makers.'"

"Aha, what's so special about the cheese makers?"

"Well, obviously it's not meant to be taken literally; it refers to any manufacturers of dairy products" (H/T Monty Python, *Life of Brian*).

As hearers and readers in another time we can only be confronted by the strange new world of the Bible (#KarlBarth). Apocalyptic literature challenges us to cultivate the heart of a prophet and the imagination of a poet in order to

THE DEACON

You might be a theology nerd if you use a Barth hashtag.

understand how the Bible often dances between metaphor, image, and symbol. This dance opens us to worlds we don't usually inhabit. It allows us to cultivate the imagination to move between past and present. It's not an easy dance, and some interpreters (I'm looking at you, Tim LaHaye) are so clumsy they'll never make it onto "Dancing with God." They can't avoid projecting onto the Bible their crumpled bundle of fears, anxieties, and hopes.

Our political, social, and even aesthetic worlds are found in these strange texts of fearsome flying beasts, angelic hosts, and lambs. New readings of apocalyptic texts throughout Christian history have offered both chaos and wisdom. The most sublime hopes and vulgar desires have found inspiration in these writings. Apocalypses challenge us. When our allegiances are called into question by Revelation's hard simplicity of choosing the woman or the dragon, we struggle to respond. Babylon may well be located in the deep recesses of my heart, influencing my life in ways little suspected. What is sobering to realize is how much our interpretations reflect the sensitivities and habits of thought that have shaped us.

Ancient texts contain revelation, though not in the way that fundamentalism understands the term. Without these texts our memory is in danger of dissipating over time. More than that, the internal world of what we imagine to be possible is embedded within these texts. Our

world may not be one of four beasts and ten horns, of flying, winged creatures, of riders on horseback, but these
and other images in the apocalypses still find resonance
among us. One of the reasons this is the case is that biblical
apocalypses were often written by those estranged from
their world. Given the tone of the 2016 presidential race in
America, alienation, like love, is still all around us.

Jewish apocalyptic writings coincided with three
great national traumas: exile into Babylon (587/6 BCE), the
oppression of the Seleucid ruler Antiochus IV (176 BCE),
and the destruction of Jerusalem (70 CE). It's difficult to see
God's plan when your nation has fallen apart, your people
have been exiled to foreign lands, and the great symbol
(the temple) of your religious world razed to the ground.
We all need some hope when our identity is under assault.
When we find antagonistic attitudes toward the political
powers that influence people's lives in these writings we
nod our heads, knowing the disappointment of leaders
failing us. If we perceive ourselves on the margins, or find
ourselves suspicious of the surrounding culture's values,
it's comforting to read that one day the reversals shall come
and we'll no longer suffer from the oppression of others.
Visions that are exotic and rich with meaning inspire us
when we feel we live in a visionless world. Apocalypses
offer us the hope of a new heaven, a new earth, and, above
all, the seduction of vindication. This was as true for the
authors of Daniel as it is for us.

Daniel, My Brother, You Are Older Than Me

As a part of apocalyptic literature, the book of Daniel
looms large. It's unique in the Hebrew Bible as the only

true apocalypse; though similar eschatological themes show up in other prophets. Dispensationalists are skillful at taking the book of Daniel and weaving an easily understood narrative out of it, but this can only be done if you don't accept that the social worlds from which the Bible emerges are important. Ignoring historical context is like making a cake, only you forget to use the sugar, eggs, icing, and flavoring; basically anything that makes the cake worth eating. Your viscous lump of flour and milk is an #EpicFail. Creating apocalyptic scenarios that ignore the world that gave rise to those images is just like that cake—wholly your own creation, but it looks and tastes awful.

Maybe you remember Daniel from your days in Sunday school, or as I like to refer to it, "doing time." In between cutting off Daniel's head and sticking it into the lion's mouth on the felt-covered board in my classroom, I heard stories of Daniel, lions, and weird writing, but the book is actually about a lot more than that. Daniel itself is a compilation of texts, with biblical scholars drawing a distinction between chapters 1–6 and 7–12. The Daniel of the first six chapters, what are known as the court stories, "operates as a Babylonian wise man, skilled in the interpretation of dreams."[3] Though set in Babylon during the exile, the author's knowledge of Babylonian and Persian history is flawed with erroneous dates and rulers.[4] In Daniel 1–6 we have an optimistic view of foreign rule as Daniel triumphs over corruption, showing how Jews can function in a Gentile world. The stories of Daniel in the lion's den with the three figures standing with him, the writing on the wall, or Nebuchadnezzar's dream and Daniel's interpretation are familiar to many of us, but the important part of the story is that Daniel was faithful, even to the point of winning the king's respect.

This is the world of *political prophecy*, where God manages the universe and even those entities that threaten God's people are instruments God uses to accomplish divine purposes, even when those powers become rebellious monsters. Stories of Jewish relations to Gentile kings run through both major sections of Daniel, but things take a turn with chapter 7, which moves to more visionary imagery and apocalyptic tones.

There's a consensus that the second part of Daniel can be dated around 165 BCE, during the time of the Seleucid dynasty and the reign of Antiochus IV, sometimes referred to as Epiphanes ("manifestation of Zeus"), a notoriously brutal ruler who had no respect for the religious sensitivities of his subjects. It was Antiochus who touched off the crisis that gave birth to Daniel 7–12 by installing an altar to Zeus in the Jewish temple, leading to the revolt of the Maccabees from 167 to 160 BCE. This period was not simply a case of Jew against Greek, but Jew against Jew, as some Jews collaborated with the Hellenists and Antiochus. Under the shadow of Antiochus IV those Jews who didn't collaborate were persecuted, even killed, for maintaining their identity against the forced acceptance of Hellenistic idolatry.

In the midst of this life-and-death conflict, Daniel uses familiar elements of traditional apocalyptic writings for ideological purposes to heighten the sense of urgency against the designs of Antiochus and his collaborators within the Jewish community. In Daniel's hands the historical particularity of the present crisis was obscured and assimilated into a cosmic pattern, and his visions can be reapplied as circumstances warrant. But for Daniel the outcome of oppression is inevitable; God will judge the oppressor and deliver God's people.

THE DEACON

Why wasn't this in my teen study Bible?

Whew! That's a lot to absorb, but I hope you get the point. You can't ignore this information if you want to truly understand what Daniel means for us today, but this is where many of the prophecy folks go a bit wiggy (I'm sure that's a theological term in some universe). They use obscure texts to tease out an interpretation to fit their particular scheme. Where Daniel uses numbers like seventy years, seventy weeks, 1260 days, forty-two months, or three and a half years to signal that there will be an end to Antiochus's reign, prophecy hucksters proclaim this is all code for some specified time to come in the future. Daniel uses specific times to comfort those caught in the midst of oppression by telling them that Antiochus has an expiration date. He's not forecasting The End. Of course, for those committed to this interpretation, they'll never give it up. Just like those who claim that the unemployment rate is higher in 2015 than it was in 2009, or that Jar Jar Binks was an awesome character. Some beliefs are resistant to facts.

Take the seventh chapter of Daniel, with its images of beasts and horns, for example. Daniel uses the imagery to challenge the authority of Antiochus IV, but it's also the part of Daniel that holds the most fascination for prophecy buffs, because they can read pretty much anything they want into it. Hal Lindsey called it "The Greatest Chapter in the Old Testament." Lindsey dismisses the scholarly consensus on the book as coming from unbelievers who love to tear the Book of Daniel apart: "Some liberal professors claim that it was written in 165 B.C., in order to discredit the supernatural element of prophecy."[5] Well, then, we wouldn't want to let a little thing like scholarly opinion stand in the way of our fantasies would we? This is one of those places where we put God in our box, developing a theory of biblical inspiration and interpretation that has to function "just so." If Daniel is not predictive, it loses authority. Damn liberal professors.

Personally I try to avoid having the truth get in the way of a good story.

THE ELDER

In these writings Daniel is addressing the struggles his people are enduring, and his response to Antiochus is couched in imagery from other Jewish and non-Jewish apocalypses that also have visions of four beasts. This four-kingdom scheme originated in Near Eastern resistance to Greek and Roman rule, but the writer of Daniel obviously borrows from these traditions to set his tale.[6] The beasts/kingdoms/horns Daniel uses all speak to the same thing—empires come and go, but God's people prevail. It's a good message, maybe even one we need to hear today.

Okay, time for a break. Go get a drink, take a bathroom stop, go for a walk. You might be wondering, "What does any of this absolutely fascinating background have to do with whether Russia is going to invade Israel, a third temple is going to be built in Jerusalem, or who the Antichrist is? This is the stuff I really want to know." We're getting to that, so patience.

THE DEACON

Nicolae Carpathia?
#LeftBehind

Daniel's images of beasts, sea, and horns have been employed over the years to mark whatever powers the persecuted community was dealing with, much like those in the present age identify these symbols with current enemies. This fluidity is what gives apocalypses their enormous power to shape our imaginations. Successive generations could read anything in these texts they wanted. Early Christians read Rome into Daniel's final beast, probably with good reason as we shall see, and many continue to read into the text ideas that Daniel did not intend to convey.

This is most certainly the case when dispensationalists identify Jesus with Daniel's "Son of Man." The fact that Jesus uses "Son of Man" imagery and even identifies himself as the "Son of Man" has created no few pages of scholarship, but this is a complicated term, used in ancient literature in several different ways. In Daniel, the "Son of Man" is a heavenly figure who fights for Israel against the empires that seek to dominate God's people. In the following chapters of Daniel it's Michael the archangel who will do battle for Israel, leading some to identify the "Son of Man" with Michael. The "Son of Man" also shows up in other apocalypses. In 1 Enoch 46:1, for instance, the "Son of Man" is described much like in Daniel; he has the appearance of a man and his face is full of graciousness, like one of the holy angels.[7] The point is that "the Son of Man" doesn't have one meaning in scripture, but several different meanings over time. Jesus doesn't really appear in Daniel, though you'd never know that from the current crop of prophecy "experts."

God Wins!

While the identity of one like the "Son of Man" is interesting to speculate about, the most important aspect of this passage is the unveiling that takes place. On earth things may look dire. Jews beset by enemies from within and without are in peril, obedience to God leads to persecution and death, but in the heavenly realm God and the angelic hosts fight for Israel. Despite the power of earthly empires, in the end God will overthrow all those who oppose God's people. To accept the idea that the authorities who rule over you should be resisted in the name of a higher authority threatens the empire. It's a profoundly subversive notion. If this is a correct way to read Daniel (and I believe it is), we find a compelling narrative of faith's radical patience in the face of persecution.

This need for radical waiting is also found in the ninth chapter of Daniel, a chapter that holds lurid fascination for dispensationalists because they locate the Antichrist in its images and metaphors. When I was in the Children of God, this was one of those places where people would freak out the most trying to identify the Antichrist with some current figure. ("It's Nixon, I'm sure of it." "No, you're wrong, I'm sure it's Brezhnev; no American can be the Antichrist; it has to be a commie.") You can only think this way if you assume Daniel is referring to the Antichrist, which he isn't. That's because the Antichrist isn't there, no matter how hard dispensationalists try to make that fit into their understanding of the "prince who is to come" (Daniel 9:26).

Daniel writes that this prince who is to come shall make a covenant with many for one week (7 years), but after half of the week (three and a half years) he shall make sacrifice and offering cease: and in their place shall be an abomination that desolates, until the decreed end is poured upon the desolator (Daniel 9:27). Placed in the context of Daniel, scholars believe that Onias III, a well-regarded priest who was murdered in 171 BCE, is a likely candidate for the anointed one Daniel speaks of in verse 9:26. If this is the case, then the seven-year period concludes in 164 BCE, a year or two after the text is composed. The writer has the end of the oppressive reign of Antiochus in sight; he's telling his readers that the tyrant's days are numbered.

We shall see later how this passage of Daniel 9:24–27 becomes, in the hands of dispensationalists, a literal rendering of events at the end of the world, where the Antichrist will make a deal with Jews in Israel to rebuild the temple, but after three and a half years he'll betray them and demand that his image stand in the rebuilt temple, signaling the final countdown (#Europe) to the end of the world. This is the scenario portrayed in the *Left Behind* series, and taught by most dispensational teachers and speakers. But there's no reason to see this as a legitimate interpretation of Daniel's words outside of a preconceived scheme that millions of people have been talked into accepting.

If Daniel was written to counter political oppression, we have a window into what this story meant and how important it was in giving encouragement to people who dealt with great persecution. In the ancient world the priority of the gods over earthly affairs was assumed. The larger reality was spiritual, not physical. The battle between Jews and Greeks would be portrayed as a battle between their heavenly patrons, which is certainly the case in the later chapters of Daniel. I heard this perspective in the Children of God. They said that every city had its own spirit, and each city's life reflected the spirit behind it. I got an earful about what the spirit of New York City represented, but, to be fair, it was the early seventies, and Times Square was a much different place. There's still prostitution—it just wears a Disney costume now.

Except for Merida and Elsa.

THE ACOLYTE

Apocalyptic literature is meant to offer hope. People with little social or military power aren't going to prevail over empires. God is going to have to fight for them. If Daniel is responding to the havoc that Antiochus creates, and he can't follow the Maccabees into their world of violence (note to self: call Mel Gibson with familiar, yet new, movie idea: *Judas Maccabeus—takes a licking and keeps on ticking*), this idea of spiritual forces having the final word in the matter makes perfect sense. We discover in the apocalypse of Daniel a world where God's chosen prevail over superior military might without taking up weapons like the Maccabees, because heaven itself is fighting for them. Daniel tells the story of a plucky band of believers who resist the forces of the empire and their evil leader ("Mr. Lucas, there's someone on line one for you; says it's about cultural appropriation"). God's defeat of an empire that sought to impose the worship of idols on Jews who did not want to assimilate into Hellenistic culture is assured to those who suffer.

Daniel let persecuted Jews know that the time of their oppression would come to an end and that their God hadn't deserted them. The truly wise knew these things, because contrary to all public evidence the outcome had been predetermined in heaven. The understanding that Jews would prevail also offers consolation for those like the Maccabees who gave their lives. This is a powerful idea. Love may not win, but God does. The idea that vindication comes no matter what, that the oppressor cannot dictate the terms of your death, cannot threaten you with annihilation and meaningless death, undercuts the tyrant's greatest threat against you.[8]

The very repetition of images in the second part of Daniel conveys that apocalypses are not claiming literal and historical truths, but through the poetic power of myth are invitations to think differently about the world. This flies in the face of those who see the Bible's authority in literal decrees or propositional revelation. The minds of the writers of these texts imagined a world where events on earth were a reflection of heavenly realities. Adopting forms and genres well known to the ancient world, Daniel narrates an interpretation of history guided by the sovereignty of God.

If the prophetic voice reveals what happens when humans choose certain courses of action over others, then Daniel serves as encouragement for those who suffer under the hands of oppressive political orders. To remove the struggles of those for whom the book was written in order to make it fit an interpretation of scripture like dispensationalism is to cram the prophecy sausage into some pretty worn skins. Still, we're faced with the reality that some of Daniel's use of numbers, or concepts like the "Son of Man" show up in the New Testament, especially in Revelation. This constancy would seem to negate my claims, so perhaps a closer look at those texts would also help our understanding.

I Got Yer Apocalypse Right Here

As he came out of the temple, one of his disciples said to him, "Look, Teacher, what large stones and what large buildings!" Then Jesus asked him, "Do you see these great buildings? Not one stone will be left here upon another; all will be thrown down."

When he was sitting on the Mount of Olives opposite the temple, Peter, James, John, and Andrew asked him privately, "Tell us, when will this be, and what will be the sign that all these things are about to be accomplished?"

Mark 13:1–4

March 22, 1973
Dear Diary,

I saw the worst horror movie last night. It was called *A Thief in the Night.* I'm not sure, but it may have cost about $3.50 to make. I'm going to write that new director

I've heard so much about, John Waters. I'm sure it'll inspire him in his film career. I've seen some pretty scary things in my life, but what that poor Patty Jo Meyers had to go through was some spooky stuff. Evidently there's this thing called the Rapture, where all the "real" believers in Jesus are taken to heaven. Patty Jo went to church, read the Bible, was actually kind of a decent person, not like most of my friends, but Jeebus, that wasn't enough to save her in the end. Poor Patty Jo wakes up one morning and finds that she's on God's cut list. Everyone she loves is gone and she's left here on earth with a bunch of jerks. Seems like a sorry thing for God to do, but that's what's so scary about it. Evidently God can be a bit cranky. Of course, the movie implies that Patty Jo doesn't really have an excuse; she brought it on herself. Serves her right for not believing the right way, I suppose.

Everyone in this movie has to get these crazy tattoos of weird lines on their hand or forehead or they can't go shopping. Man, God is such a bummer sometimes. Takes our loved ones, and then, after that, rips all meaning and purpose out of our lives. Take mom if you have to, but the shopping mall? Did I mention God is mean? Anyway, in the movie some guys from something called UNITE (the United Nations doesn't come off good in this thing at all) chase her down trying to get her to take that goofy tattoo, but poor Patty Jo falls off a bridge and dies. Only she doesn't die; she wakes up and realizes it's all a dream. And here's where I found myself breathing really hard and sweating like mom at night (at least that's what she told daddy when she asked for separate beds); her radio crackles out the bad news when she wakes up—millions of people have disappeared. It's like that dream where you wake up from dreaming you're a butterfly and you're wondering if you're a human dreaming you're a butterfly, or a butterfly dreaming you're a human. Or, something like that. I don't know, but the fact that God torments her with a dream and then the real thing smacks her in the face is just wrong. I only hope they don't make any more movies about this whole Rapture thing, because this one sucked so badly I can't imagine they could get any better over time. If I were God, I'd sue for slander because I'm sure he can't be that moody. Well, going to try and sleep now and hope I don't wake up with people missing, but if they are, I hope Buffy's gone. He's so stuck up; he won't even talk to me.

Yours truly, the ever-awesome Stacy

Sign, Sign, Everywhere a Sign

This diary could've been written by countless kids who went to church youth group not suspecting that youth pastor Billy Ray Jim Bob ("you can call me Bubba for short") had cued up the church's VCR with a movie that would scare the bejeesus out of them. Right after the movie they might've been encouraged to open their Bible to Mark

---

Did your church host the traveling "scare 'em to Jesus" dramatic production *Heaven's Gate Hell's Flame?* #BeJesusExplosion.

THE DEACON

---

where they'd find that Jesus' friends sure did put the "duh" in disciples. The thing is; we're a lot like those disciples. We all want a sign, a little bit of a heads up. It would help us prepare ourselves if we knew what the future held. It's hard to live in the moment and trust God. According to some biblical interpreters, we have a detailed forecast from Jesus himself what our future looks like in Mark 13 and Matthew 24, known as the "Small Apocalypses." These texts, drawing on imagery from Daniel and other Jewish apocalypses, have formed the backbone of prophetic interpretation for millennia. Since they were written as expressing Jesus' own thoughts on the matter, many see in these passages the confirmation of their end times scenarios.

According to Mark 13—the earliest of the apocalypses in the Gospels—the contours of the end of the world are roughly: The Temple of Jerusalem will be destroyed (v. 2), a series of signs will unfold such as wars (v. 7), famine, earthquakes, and social upheaval (v. 8), and natural disasters (vv. 24–25). Despite the persecution of those who bear witness to Jesus, the "good news" will be proclaimed to all the nations (vv. 9–10). At some point during all this turmoil the "desolating sacrilege" (v. 14) sets up "where it ought not to be"—which, if you live in Judea, is time to head for the hills. During these days there will be false messiahs and false prophets who will deceive many (v. 22). This is a time of great tribulation, which, if not cut short, would destroy life on earth; God is gracious, however, and cuts the days short on behalf of the elect (v. 20). After all this suffering, the Son of Man will come in clouds with great power and glory and gather his elect from the ends of the earth to go to heaven (vv. 26–27).

This is roughly the story line that the Gospel of Mark follows concerning the end of the world, a narrative that also bears striking resemblance to other Jewish apocalypses, right down to the phrasing. For example, in 4 Ezra, a text contemporaneous with the first century, we read of similar times of great trial and tribulation with some of the same disasters, earthquakes, turmoil, and "nation rising up against nation" (4 Ezra 13:30ff.) until the "one whom the Most High has been keeping for generations" will appear to reprove the assembled nations for their ungodliness (4 Ezra 13:37–38). Given the similarity between these writings, it seems clear that Mark drew on literature known by him to strengthen his teaching.

In Matthew's version of this passage he takes the entirety of Mark's rendering, but also, because he has his own theological interests and other material to work with, adds his distinctive perspective. For example, one of Matthew's additions has become a classical text used by dispensationalists to argue the case for the Rapture: "Then two will be in the field; one will be taken, one will be left. Two women will be grinding meal together; one will be taken and one will be left. Keep awake therefore, for you do not know on what day your Lord is coming" (Matthew 24:40–42).

A closer look at the verses preceding these two reveals that Matthew is writing about the judgment that came upon the earth in Noah's time. When read in context, this means that the ones being left behind are those who escape the judgment; the ones who are taken are those who are swept away in judgment. Being left behind is actually the desirable position. To read this text in any other way is a clear misreading of the entirety of the idea in this section.

There's no Rapture in Matthew and to find one there is a complete distortion of the text. His eschatological perspective is that the return (*parousia*) of Christ will disclose who is saved and who is lost. Given that "I Wish We'd All Been Ready" was the theme song for *A Thief in the Night*, this may have confused many people trying to make sense of Matthew's take on things.

THE ELDER

You should redeem the torture of watching these things by turning them into a drinking game.

Other scholars have claimed that perhaps the concerns that Mark and Matthew addressed were much nearer to Jesus' own time. Gerd Theissen, for example, proposed that a crisis during the years 35–41 CE when the Roman Emperor Caligula demanded that a statue of him be put up in the temple precincts actually forms the backdrop behind the apocalyptic material in the Gospels. This would make more sense in identifying what the "desolating sacrilege" was, but the majority of scholars suggest an even later date for Mark.[1]

Matthew 24:15 and Mark 13:14 certainly point us to the "abomination that causes desolation," a term found in Daniel 9:27. In the hands of dispensationalists, the figure desolating the holy place can only be the Antichrist. They contend the Antichrist will put his image in the rebuilt third Temple in Jerusalem to be worshiped at the midpoint of the last seven years of the world. But if the accepted date for the writing of Mark and Matthew holds, then either no temple existed, or the future of the temple was evident at this time, so the ambiguity of "the holy place" (Matthew 24:15) or "where it ought not to be" (Mark 13:14) offers a number of different interpretations.

The "abomination that causes desolation" in Daniel 9:27 refers to an object or person who profanes the sanctuary, which fits the attempt of Antiochus IV to install his image in Jerusalem's temple. If an earlier dating of Mark is held, then commentators argue that the Roman Emperor Caligula's attempt to place his image in the temple precincts would fit this sacrilege. If a later date is accurate, then some scholars suggest that perhaps the desecration of the temple during the Zealots' revolt is the reference. It's reasonable to assume that these verses reflect the struggles of a generation after Jesus, and the original readers would have read them as prophecy that had been fulfilled. Interestingly, Luke 21:20–24 dispenses with the whole figure of the "desolating sacrilege" altogether, suggesting that the whole issue of the temple is moot by that point.

Dispensationalists claim that the verses about the "desolating sacrilege" are about the Antichrist setting up his image in the rebuilt Temple of Jerusalem, but the Antichrist is nowhere mentioned in any apocalyptic passage of the Gospels. Because dispensationalists read this figure into Daniel 9, they refuse to accept the fact that Daniel is speaking of the struggle Jews faced with Antiochus IV and Matthew and Mark are referring to events in their time. When a grid of interpretation is laid on the Bible in order to conform to preconceived schemes, we miss some important things.

Son of Man Redux

The basic storyline in Mark 13, Matthew 24, and Luke 21 reflects some of the concerns of earlier Jewish apocalypses. Those Jewish texts tell of a time when Jerusalem and Israel will be restored (a given for Paul). Israel's restoration was much on the minds of the disciples after 70 CE. But we also find another figure that had a long history in Jewish apocalyptic writings, the Son of Man, who Jesus says will come in the clouds with great power and glory. This brings us to one of the most complex set of questions about these apocalyptic passages: Who was the Son of Man Jesus refers to in these passages? Is he the Messiah? Was Jesus predicting his own return?

Eyes rolling back into your head? Okay, wonk warning—we're going a bit into the weeds, but it's important to have all the facts, otherwise you'll find yourself on city streets grabbing strangers and telling them that the fourth blood moon really is a sign of the last days. Grab another hot

THE ACOLYTE

I doubt you can go deep enough in the weeds for this . . .

pocket and a beer, or a bowl of kale chips and hang in there for a bit longer. No one ever said theology was easy.

There can be no doubt that the eschatological proclamation of the kingdom of God was a central part of Jesus' ministry. Starting with his baptism by the apocalyptically oriented figure of John the Baptist, Jesus' teachings

Personally I think kale chips pair well with some Red Stripe. Ok it did once, but don't tell anyone.

THE BISHOP

continually announced that the kingdom of God was at hand. This was such a revolutionary claim that Jesus inaugurated his ministry by reading from Isaiah 61: "The Spirit of the Lord is upon me, because he has anointed me to bring good news to the poor. He has sent me to proclaim release to the captives and recovery of sight to the blind, to let the oppressed go free, to proclaim the year of the Lord's favor" (Luke 4:18–19).

Jesus believed he would play a central role in the coming reign of God, but Jesus' understanding of his role in God's new age doesn't necessarily align with how the term "Messiah" was understood. In fact, the concept of the Messiah was a very fluid term from the time it appears in apocalyptic literature. In some versions the Messiah is a conquering warrior who will restore the fortunes of Israel, but this wasn't a universal understanding. In the Similitudes of Enoch, the Son of Man is referred to as a messiah and his coming is linked to the resurrection of the dead.[2] This title was given to Jesus shortly after his death, the word "Christ" being the Greek equivalent of "messiah." But Jesus actually fit in more with the Similitude of Enoch's description than Daniel's conquering warrior who fights for Israel.

How did the gospel writers envision the image of the Son of Man found in Daniel? "Son of Man" was a notoriously difficult idea to pin down. We saw in the previous chapter that this figure may have been associated with the archangel Michael who fights for the Jews in Daniel 10–12, but when Jesus refers to himself as the Son of Man, we cannot use angelic figures to identify the Son of Man.

To complicate the situation, mentions of the Son of Man in the Gospels are varied. Sometimes Jesus uses the term in a nonapocalyptic way, as in "Foxes have holes and birds of the air have nests, but the Son of Man has nowhere to lay his head" (Matthew 8:20; Luke 9:58); but in other passages the Son of Man is an apocalyptic figure—the instrument of God's coming judgment, fitting in more with the figure in Daniel, who also comes on clouds. This meshes with other places in the Gospels where Jesus identifies as the Son of Man who possesses unique authority to forgive sins, or is the Lord of the Sabbath.

Scholars such as the previously mentioned John Collins point out that "the Son of Man" is most likely a distinction given to Jesus post-resurrection. This identification of Jesus with Daniel's Son of Man would make sense given the fact that the messianic figure of Daniel delivers the people of Israel from oppression. The coming again on clouds, mirroring Daniel's Son of Man, meant that the early church anticipated the completion of Christ's work.

This is a complicated topic, and scholarly opinion is not set. Given that Jesus did not fit the mold of the warrior king who would drive out the Gentiles, the disciples found a path to interpret Daniel in a way that would fit their experience of the resurrected Jesus: "Consequently, after his death the disciples searched the scriptures for an explanation of this surprising turn of events. Daniel's prophecy provided them with a different model of the Messiah, and they concluded that Jesus would come again, not as an earthly king but as the Danielic Son of Man on the clouds of heaven."[3]

This conclusion of the first followers of Jesus—that he would soon return as the heavenly ruler who gathers his elect—would establish the path forward for the rest of church history. We presently stand at the end of that long path and over two thousand years of speculation about what the return of Christ means. But it wasn't only the Gospel authors who struggled with Jesus' finishing what he started; other biblical writers also wrestled with the return of Christ.

Was Paul Wrong?

Yes! At least about patriarchy, slavery, the generational arrival of Jesus' return, and

THE ELDER

his insistence tweezers can't help remove thorns from the flesh.

The anticipation of Christ's return infuses the rest of the New Testament. Flipping open the Bible, one is greeted by such passages as:

- "The end of all things is near; therefore be serious and discipline yourselves for the sake of your prayers." (1 Peter 4:7)

- "Since all these things are to be dissolved in this way, what sort of persons ought you to be in leading lives of holiness and godliness, waiting for and hastening the coming of the day of God, because of which the heavens will be set ablaze and dissolved, and the elements will melt with fire?" (2 Peter 2:11–12)

- "As to the coming of our Lord Jesus Christ and our being gathered together to him, we beg you, brothers and sisters, not to be quickly shaken in mind or alarmed, either by spirit or by word or by letter, as though from us, to the effect that the day of the Lord is already here." (2 Thessalonians 2:1–2)

- "Children, it is the last hour! As you have heard that antichrist is coming, so now many antichrists have come. From this we know that it is the last hour." (1 John 2:18)

Sometimes the writers of the New Testament sound as if the coming of Christ could happen at any second; at other times there are warnings that the faithful are in it for the long haul and they should expect a lot of difficulty in the interim. Intense speculation and caution can exist in the same text as the writers try to read the times. New Testament writings reflect this ambiguity depending on the circumstances in which they originated. There can be no doubt that the anticipation of Christ's return was a part of the early church's faith.

If you're still here, that means you're okay thinking about the wonky stuff, right? Or have you just skimmed these last few pages, because, you know, Bible stuff is hard? It's especially hard when we have to say that someone like Paul was . . . well . . . wrong. There's no question that Paul, along with the rest of the church, awaited the imminent coming of Jesus. He also swam in the apocalyptic pool, even to the point of sharing the genre's vision of a heavenly journey: "I know a man in Christ who fourteen years ago was caught up to the third heaven—whether in the body or out of the body I do not know, God knows. And I know that this man was caught up into Paradise . . . and he heard things that cannot be told, which man may not utter" (2 Corinthians 12:2–4).

In one of the earliest writings of the New Testament, 1 Thessalonians, composed around 50 CE, Paul expects a quick return of Jesus. He cautions the church that the day of the Lord would come like a thief in the night (5:2), but they will at least be prepared because they were children of light not darkness. Immediately before this admonition we find another of those passages that have become so central to dispensational belief in the Rapture:

> But we do not want you to be uninformed, brothers and sisters, about those who have died, so that you may grieve as others do who have no hope. For since we believe that Jesus died and rose again, even so, through Jesus, God will bring with him those who have died. For this we declare to you by the word of the Lord, that we who are alive will by no means precede those who have died.

> For the Lord himself, with a cry of command,
> with the archangel's call and with the sound of
> God's trumpet, will descend from heaven, and
> the dead in Christ will rise first. Then we who
> are alive, who are left, will be caught up into the
> clouds together with them to meet the Lord in
> the air; and so we will be with the Lord forever.
> Therefore encourage one another with these
> words. (1 Thessalonians 4:13–18)

How could it be any clearer? We will be "caught up
into the clouds" to meet the Lord in the air. It's right there
in black and white. Or, at least that's what I used to tell
people when I was nineteen and just caught wind of *A
Thief in the Night*.

Only it's not as clear as those who believe in the Rapture
think it is. Throughout his letter to the Thessalonian community Paul clearly indicates that he believes the return of
Jesus is imminent, and as is the case with all biblical texts,
he has a number of Jewish apocalypses at hand to use for
the imagery of angels, trumpets of God, and "those who
are left." In the larger context of the letter, Paul is addressing the resurrection of the dead at Christ's second coming
and consoling the church that they will not be separated
from those who have already died because they also will
resurrect to new life. The letter is meant to comfort believers whose loved ones had died by assuring them that the
return of Christ would not leave out those who had died.

But according to the believers in the Rapture, what
we find in this passage is that Jesus comes, takes people
to heaven for seven years (or if you're a mid-Tribulation

Rapture kind of believer, for three-and-a-half years), and then comes back . . . again. At the sound of God's trumpet the Lord descends from heaven to take his own, first the dead and then we who are alive who will be "caught up in the clouds." What could be more obvious that this is the Rapture? But, according to the dispensationalists, Christ snatches the true believers (which doesn't include bad believers like Patty Jo, or apostate pastors like Bruce Barnes in *Left Behind*) and takes them to heaven (Jesus in full Schwarzenegger mode: "I'll be baaack!") until he *really* returns seven years later. Where is the mention of seven years in this text? Does the Lord reverse course, coming halfway and then turn around when the dead and believers have risen to meet him? Dispensationalists argue this verse has to be placed in the larger context of their interpretive grid, but this is part of the problem with a system that crams the Bible into a preconceived mold. This passage reflects Paul's belief in the imminent return of Christ and the resurrection of the dead that will happen at that time, not a secret coming seven years before Jesus comes to finish his business.

If we pull the lens back a bit, we find that the writers of the New Testament are trying to work out theologically the growing tension between the quickly returning Christ and the felt experience of a too-long delay. One of the ways they did this was to place the resurrection at the heart of Christian teaching. The fact that the early church understood Jesus as the Son of Man who comes on clouds to gather believers presupposes the belief that he was risen and ascended.[4] The resurrection becomes the central eschatological moment in the New Testament. Working out the belief that the reign of God was at hand, with the ongoing struggles of life, the church came to believe that the new age had already begun in some sense.

That the already of the new age can exist alongside expectation of Christ returning in Paul's lifetime is reflected in an earlier passage (1 Corinthians 7:29–31) where Paul tells the church at Corinth that the time is so close it makes no sense to carry on life as normal. If you're not married, don't get married; if you don't own things don't start shopping now, things are wrapping up. If Paul were writing today he'd say don't plan on going to *Star Wars* VIII. Heck, you were lucky enough to get VII, which should've helped with forgetting *The Phantom Menace*.

THE ELDER

After hearing about the Rapture-inspired fiction it makes Jar Jar only slightly painful.

Paul's expectations here are not out of line with other New Testament writers. As time passes and it dawns on the first community of Jesus' followers that his anticipated return may not take place in their lifetimes, the landscape shifts a bit. The church had to discern the promised reign of God through a lens that grew ever more opaque. This tension between the already of Jesus' resurrection and the not yet of John's Revelation constitutes one of the perennial struggles of Christian faith. Millions of Christians place their hope and faith in the soon returning Lord, while others believe that the promised new age is a present reality for those with the heart to believe it. Perhaps a look at the mother of all apocalypses can clear this all up for us.

So what if you're a Christian who thinks Jesus coming back at all seems weird? It all seems far-fetched.

THE ACOLYTE

4

Of Whores and Beasts

Fantastic Stories and amazing predictions that the apocalypse was near began to circulate among the people. Charlatans and self-appointed prophets roamed the streets prophesying whatever came into their heads and terrifying the majority of the people. . . . Society never fails to throw up a bewildering variety of such people in times of misfortune.

Agathias, *Historiarum libri quinque*,
sixth century

Visitors to Rome often experience the breathtaking moment of coming out of the subway stop at the Colosseum and being overwhelmed by the sight of the enormous, magnificent ruins across the street. The Colosseum projects strength even as it decays into a tourist attraction and home for feral cats. How much more Rome must have seemed to those who lived under its domain. It was unassailable, resistance was futile; which makes the imagination of the writer of Revelation even more remarkable, for he has the boldness at the end of the first century to forecast Rome's demise.

It's surely more fascinating to see the book of Revelation as a code for the end of the world than a work of apocalyptic literature written for first-century Christians. We can, like Tim LaHaye or John Hagee, endlessly speculate about so many things: how modern weapons can be burned; whether the number of the Beast is coming from a computer in Brussels, or a computer chip that will be implanted in our hands to be scanned; if Barack Obama is the Antichrist; whether the ten horns of the beast's head is the United Nations Security Council, or who is the whore in chapter 17. It's fun to play biblical jerk-a-verse, but the broad brush I'm using to pull out major themes and raise critical questions paints another picture. What it lacks in morbid curiosity about the end of the world, however, may reveal an even more important reality as we think about how this strange book of images speaks to us today.

The book of Revelation was most likely written during the reign of Emperor Domitian, somewhere around 95–96 CE on the island of Patmos. Even twenty-five years after the destruction of Jerusalem, its temple, and the exile of Jews from Israel, memories were still fresh in people's minds. In our postmodern world, historical consciousness doesn't seem to extend beyond breakfast, but for John's readers the past was always lingering in the present. In the face of cultural devastation and ongoing tensions with the empire, the author of Revelation wrote an apocalypse to drive home his point that Rome was on the clock and time was running out. Though Rome exercised enormous power, it too would fall. The author obviously knows apocalyptic literature, because he borrowed from Jewish writing, especially the prophets, to construct his story.

Those influenced by dispensational perspectives believe that all prophecy is a prediction of the future, so what we have in Revelation is a blueprint for the end of the world. Revelation is one massive code that needs to be cracked for us to understand how the world will end. If we accept this argument—that the entire book was written just for our generation—we join a vast tradition almost 2,000 years running of Christians who also thought this about the times they lived in. If Revelation is not a road-map for the future, however, we have other options for interpreting it. John continually warned his readers that the things he describes in the text are soon to take place; the time is near (22:10). John wasn't forecasting a horizon far out into the future; he was writing for Christians in his day to encourage them in the face of persecution.

Apocalyptic vision and prophetic witness stand in close proximity to one another. In the prophets, events were often forecast in very general ways—the prophets saw sin in front of them and made predictions about what would happen if there was no repentance. The prophetic word claimed it had a divine window on the world: pursue your present course of oppressing widows, keeping all the wealth for yourself, turning away the foreigner, and you'll suffer judgment. If you pay more attention to king or emperor than to me, God indicates, then your society will be too weak to respond to the challenges that your enemies are bringing to your door. Think Rome will remain an unassailable power? Good luck with that. The prophetic judgment and outcome is not in doubt if there is no repentance and an end to social oppression.

Who Is Like unto Rome?

This element of prophetic witness is present in John, but time and unfamiliarity with the ancient world obscure it from us. Barbara Rossing in her book *The Rapture Exposed: The Message of Hope in the Book of Revelation*, points her readers to an interesting aspect of Rome's ethos, one certainly known to John when he wrote—the entire ideology of the Roman Empire was predicated on the worship of Victory. The goddess Victoria (Nike in Greek) decorated Roman soldiers' flags and shields. Senators burned incense to her as they entered the Senate. Statues were erected to

---

THE DEACON

So Rome was the Imperial version of Charlie Sheen. #winning is the hastag before the fall.

---

her throughout the empire. Coins were minted for her, connecting her to the economic dominance of Rome. A whole series of Roman coins minted in 71 CE depict the goddess setting up a trophy over a prostrate Jew. The message was unmistakable—Rome keeps peace through the power of its military, resistance to the empire was futile, and it would be severely punished.[1]

The Christian faced with this imperial ideology read the book of Revelation taking into account that John's fearsome beasts and odd visions had their earthly manifestations. The entire text is constructed around the challenges that the nascent church faced at that time. The great cosmic drama, enfolding both heaven and earth, so typical of all other apocalypses, presents the struggle in the starkest terms: it's the battle of good and evil. While we might be hesitant accepting such a black-and-white picture of the world, there's some truth in this starkness. We find in apocalypses that evil often works through its ability to take space in the world, whether in political or economic spheres. Every space given to evil releases an animating energy in the orders we construct to arrange our lives. Power spawns the desire to control lands, people, and minds. It's just like this in your local neighborhood homeowners' association, but the stakes are a lot lower and the people pettier. Without resistance, the orders we build in politics or economics eventually mutate and spawn totalitarianism, even if it's the soft totalitarian promise to keep us safe.

In the face of this relentless pursuit of power and space, what is salvation? Scant years after Rome had destroyed the temple, dispersed Jews throughout the empire, paraded Jews destined for slavery through the streets of Rome, and persecuted those who followed the Jew named Jesus, John offered an alternative vision where the appearance of things is not the ultimate truth—the wealth and power of Rome will not ultimately prevail.

Rome's worship of Victory amidst daily oppression constituted the life of those who first heard and read John's text. The constant confrontation with a relentless power that narrows and proscribes life wears the oppressed down. Against this foe and its claims on life, John's winged creature responds: "Fear God . . . and worship the One who made heaven and earth." Whatever mysteries and codes contemporary interpreters may think exist in the book of Revelation, the original readers of that text knew that they were reading a subversive challenge to Roman power.

This would have been clear to all those who existed under the shadow of the empire. When eyes went to the goddess Victory on her pedestal, and crowds proclaimed, "Who is like unto Rome?" an alternative community of readers and hearers of Revelation had an answer— "Worthy is the Lamb who was slain, to receive power and wealth and wisdom and strength and honor and glory and praise" (Revelation 5:12).

How can we translate the subversive power of this into our age? American Christians might get a feel of it if they started to question the idolatries found in American exceptionalism. Think for a minute what it would be like if someone showed up at the gates of the White House and proclaimed: "Woe to you America! You have killed millions in your desire to be an empire! Woe to you for pouring your love into weapons of destruction and obscene military budgets while your poor sleep in the streets! Woe to you who call yourself innocent and good while pursuing the spirit of destruction in the name of order!" Chances are we would do with them what Rome did with those who questioned its power: throw them into prison and forget them (America *is* exceptionally good at building prisons). Those rare prophetic communities in our country who question American actions annoy and irritate the principalities and powers.

John addressed his message to the alternative community established by the Lamb. His immediate audience was the seven churches mentioned in chapters 2–3,

A tension for denominational leaders is the reality of the unjust prison system

THE BISHOP

and the defensiveness of so many church goers.

but by virtue of its inclusion into the canon of Christian scripture, Revelation is a letter to all those who follow Jesus. Though it's near impossible to re-create what the situation of those named communities in Revelation was actually like, we're told of their distinguishing character-istics. Some, like Smyrna and Philadelphia, were weak and fallible; others, like Laodicea and Pergamum, were complacent and compromised. The addresses to the angels of the churches catalogue certain attitudes and habits that identify all communities of faith through time, but all the churches do have one thing in common: they struggled with how much accommodation is pos-sible with the culture.

Compromise doesn't happen in a vacuum. How to maintain faith in the midst of dominant political power rests at the heart of Revelation. For example, Pergamum was the center of the cult of the emperor, which John describes as the place "where Satan's throne is" (Revela-tion 2:13). The worship of the state places us in the realm of the demonic. The message to this church was to resist worshiping the emperor like all their neighbors did:

"Hey Atticus, wanna come with us to the lighting of the torches festival tonight? We're going to burn some incense to Caesar."

"No thanks Marcus, I'm staying in tonight and reading scripture."

"You treasonous weirdo, why can't you be like the rest of us on the block? I'll be sure and let the neighborhood association know you're not joining in. They may want to have a word with you about your lawn."

In the midst of a hostile world, not to participate in the life of the community would've been seen as subversive. The message of an imminent salvation would've been an encouragement for those who faced such communal hostility.

Metaphors Gone Wild

What follows these letters to the churches can only be called a riot of images and metaphors, each colliding into one another. A Lamb (with a capital L) is worshiped, scrolls are opened, trumpets are sounded, dreaded horsemen are set loose, and utter destruction rains down on earth. Rome with its military and economic power is no match for this Lamb, who reverses all human values about what power means. This isn't the cute little lamb that some churches use to grace their nativity scenes for drive-bys on Christmas Eve. This lamb kicks ass, which makes one wonder about whether we've all been hoodwinked by the "sweet baby Jesus" who grows up to admonish us to love our enemies.

Part of the power of John's vision is that this is not a harmless lamb. We may have memories of pasted pictures on church school walls of Jesus holding lambs in his arms,

but this Lamb resists domestication. It's the Lamb who
unleashes the power of the four horsemen of the Apocalypse and the subsequent shaking of earthly order (Revelation 6:14–15). It's hard to escape the idea that John was
judging the failures of the economic and political orders
and the oppression they bring. It would certainly be an
understandable response. If we feel oppressed we hope the
day of reversal will come, that justice will out, and our
enemies will be vanquished. Hollywood couldn't exist if
this wasn't a narrative that tapped into deep human experience (#HarryPotter; #LordoftheRings; #HungerGames).
If we read Revelation and don't grasp the attraction of
vindication, we miss the horrible shadow that this text has
cast over human history. People inspired by Revelation
have caused massive death and destruction because they
decided to become "God's little helpers" and take matters
into their own hands.

The Lamb's wrath shocks us and, unless we thirst
for the deaths of our enemies, we struggle to reconcile
the mayhem and destruction unleashed in Revelation
with the Lamb of God who willingly gives up his life.
Did we get Jesus wrong? In Revelation, love doesn't seem
to win (sorry, @realrobbell). We who speak of love winning in the end must come to grips with these horrors and
the untold misery that ensues. Revelation has been used
throughout centuries to justify our hatreds and our secret
love of violence. Apocalyptic texts have served as inspiration throughout history for the cleansing of others from
the earth (#Münster1534).

If there is any truth to the idea that God often functions as a projection of our deepest fears, desires, and
hopes, the book of Revelation confronts us with whether

THE ACOLYTE

I am glad Wikipedia helped me decipher that hashtag. Pretty sure that story deserves a series on HBO.

we secretly want the death of our enemies. We're talking massive destruction here. A third of the earth dies: water, air, land, trees, grass (sorry about those of you in the 'burbs, but at least your Saturdays will be free now, what with all the burned-up lawns), even people—gone! Maybe the number's a metaphor, but John was not messing around. Revelation brings us to the brink of the abyss. Come quickly thug Jesus![2]

This pattern of confusion and destruction at the time of judgment is not unique to John's Revelation. Other apocalypses also speak of great tribulations before the coming of the messianic kingdom. One apocalypse, circulating in the first century, puts it like this:

> Now concerning the signs: Behold the days are coming when those who dwell on earth shall be seized with great terror, and the way of truth shall be hidden, and the land shall be barren of faith, and unrighteousness shall be increased beyond what you yourself see, and beyond what you heard of formerly. And the land which you now see ruling shall be waste and untrodden, and men shall see it desolate. But if the Most High grants that you live, you shall see it thrown into

confusion after the third period; and the sun shall
suddenly shine forth at night, and the moon during the day. Blood shall drip from wood, and
the stone shall utter its voice; the people shall be
troubled, and the stars shall fall. (4 Ezra 5:1–4)

There were so many writings of this nature circulating when Revelation was written that it starts to resem-
ble the scene in Monty Python's *Life of Brian* where the
prophets and seers are lined up along a street, each proclaiming their own unique path of destruction (Google
"crazy prophets, Monty Python style" and watch the clip;
it was probably just like that).

In the midst of opening seals, unrolling scrolls, and
sounding trumpets, we find in Revelation 11 the story
of the two witnesses who prophesy during the forty-two
months that the holy city is trampled underfoot (11:2–3).
The beast that comes up from the bottomless pit kills the
witnesses and their bodies lie in the street. The inhabitants
of the earth celebrate their deaths with parties and gift-
giving because the witnesses had tormented them. After
three-and-a-half days they get up, terrifying the onlookers,
and ascend to heaven, at which time the city experiences a
great earthquake, the second woe (Revelation 11:13).

I've always been fascinated by the two witnesses, especially by the fact that they tormented the inhabitants of the
earth so much that people felt compelled to give gifts and
celebrate their death. What would that Hallmark card
even look like?

Ding dong, the prophets are gone
A pain in our ass taken away
Let's all celebrate their much-deserved fate
And get wasted later today

What, possibly, could the two witnesses have said that would've been so tormenting? Was it like Rush Limbaugh on steroids? Elizabeth Warren dressing down Jamie Dimon? Perhaps the two witnesses said something like this: "The entirety of your constructed world, from your politics to economies, even your religion, is built on a lie. You've built kingdoms of power and violence on the oppression of others who are too vulnerable to fight back. And, worse, you did nothing to alleviate the suffering of those who were ground into dust by the empire you created. This is not the way that God intended for God's people to live. Unless you shape up, your Senate and House will turn on one another in petty bickering and viperine deceit and your empire will fall just like all the others." Oh, wait. . . . The witnesses would, of course, be accused of waging class warfare, treason, and perhaps bad taste, what with the tattered sackcloth robes and unkempt appearances, but I'm convinced that given our propensity to make God serve our tune, the message these witnesses proclaimed would still make us shpilkes.

The Woman and the Dragon

The next scene is so abrupt that it can throw us off a bit. Chapter 12 tells one of the most compelling stories in the book. It's a story of a woman and a dragon that wants to destroy her, and no, we're not talking about Daenerys Targaryen and Drogon. The woman is pregnant and the great red dragon wants to devour her child. He waits for her son to be born, but when he is, the child is snatched away to God and the woman flees the dragon's clutches, taken into the wilderness for 1,260 days (or 42 months, 3 and a half years). These times are now familiar to you, right? John was drawing on Daniel to speak of the limited period of persecution. After this, there is war in heaven and the dragon, now identified as Satan, is thrown down to earth, where he continues to pursue the woman without success (12:1–6).

Craig R. Koester, in his book *Revelation and the End of All Things*, writes that in John's time one of the stories shaping the Hellenistic world told of a fierce dragon named Python and a woman named Leto, who was the mother of the god Apollo. Leto became pregnant by Zeus and the dragon pursues her in order to kill her and her child. The north wind rescues her by bearing her to the island of Delos in the Aegean Sea where she gives birth to Apollo and Artemis. Apollo sets out in pursuit of the dragon, soon slaying the creature to avenge his mother.[3]

Identification with this story served both emperors and citizens of Rome: "[A] grateful citizen of Rome would readily think of the story as a reflection of his or her own experiences . . . the woman is the goddess Roma, the queen of heaven; the son is the emperor, who kills the dragon (the forces of chaos) and founds the new Golden Age."[4] The emperor, of course, benefits from this identification. Nero enjoyed presenting himself in the guise of Apollo, placing "his image on coins bearing the radiant beams from his head that were Apollo's trademark."[5] Christians living in that time would have known the story of the woman and the dragon and the identifications their neighbors made with the story.

John narrated a different reality. The woman, sometimes interpreted in Christian tradition as the church or the Virgin Mary, constitutes a threat to the dragon, who represents the forces seeking the destruction of Christ and his followers. Revelation takes a tale familiar to those who lived in the Greco-Roman world and subverts it in order to call into question the heavenly origins of rulers. The way John told the story, earthly rule is suspect and represents demonic forces. This truth torments those who seek power over others. In the story of the woman and the dragon, we find that the challenge to earthly power is one where Rome's version of how life should be lived is not the only life that matters. The life of faith, even if it's life in the wilderness, is always going to be a threat to those in power.

In the midst of persecution and suffering, those who do not submit overcome Satan. They may have been seen as failures by Rome, but the martyrs were not failures any more than Jesus was. Even if the dragon seems too powerful to overcome, and evil too embedded within the world to root out, resistance to the dragon is absolutely necessary. This mother who flees to the wilderness has many children, all of whom are part of God's story, but as the dragon takes his stand on the sand of the seashore, we discover that evil unwisely takes a stand on shaky foundations that are easily eroded.

THE BISHOP

That is good news that will preach.

Horns, Heads, and Fun with Numbers

Chapter 13 of Revelation occupies a special place in the heart of dispensationalism. John described a beast who rises out of the sea, with ten horns and seven heads (13:1). The horns have diadems and the heads have blasphemous names. The dragon gives the beast authority and power, even though one of its heads seemed to have a mortal wound that had been healed (13:3). The whole world worships the beast and the dragon. The beast is given power over everything for forty-two months (surprise!), causing all not written in the book of life of the Lamb to offer the beast praise (13:8).

This first beast is followed by another beast who comes from the earth and has two horns and speaks like a dragon. It exercises all the authority of the first beast on its behalf and causes the earth to worship the beast. The climax of the text comes with these verses:

> Also it causes all, both small and great, both rich and poor, both free and slave, to be marked on the right hand or the forehead, so that no one can buy or sell who does not have the mark, that is, the name of the beast or the number of its name. This calls for wisdom: let anyone with understanding calculate the number of the beast, for it is the number of a person. Its number is six hundred sixty-six. (13:16–18)

Thus begins almost two millennia of the biblical game, *Fun with Numbers*. Daniel's four beasts have here become one because this beast reflects the characteristics of the current empire, the imperial consciousness that seeks to make itself worshiped in the world. Roman emperors had authority over many tribes, people, and nations. The emperors were worshiped as gods. Tacitus, the Roman historian, tells us that some emperors encouraged being referred to as "savior" or even "son of God." The rulers had statues erected and established a cult of the emperor to solidify allegiance throughout the realm. The images speak to what really threatens the people of God—a political power that moves the world to blasphemy and rejection of God's desire for life.

The second beast that emerges from the land is a false prophet who incites the world to worship the beast, a counter to the two witnesses in chapter 11 who call the world to the truth. Craig Koester suggests that John exercised a bit of satire here. Koester relates the story of a charlatan named Alexander who "created a shrine in which he installed an image with an artificial head, whose hinged jaws could be raised and lowered by means of a system of cords. A small tube was inserted into the back of the head so that as the jaws moved, someone behind the scenes could talk through the tube and create the illusion that the idol was speaking." Koester thinks that John is mocking the image of the beast with this puppet prophet. Satire is often a clever way of poking the pretensions of the powerful, and the false prophet is a bit of a fool.[6]

As John's story continues, everyone is sealed for either the Lamb or the beast. In Revelation everyone belongs to someone. Though these marks may not be visible, they reflect the choices we all make. In the earlier part of Revelation, in the letters to the churches, the economy looms large in the churches of Laodicea and Smyrna. No matter the age we live in, we're are not immune from economic pressures, or the temptations that accompany economic power. To advance in the society of John's day would be to enter into the structures of the empire. If a local trade guide included meals offered to idols or made statues to serve in the temples, it would be hard to avoid participating, especially if you had a family:

"Hey Josephus, you see Mykros the other day? Yeah, 'lil punter; we're all throwing our sacrificed meat onto Caesar's altar, but he and his friends think they're too good for that. Little Lord Mithras, that one, if you take my meaning."

"That lot's always been self-righteous, but he'll get his. The boys tell me they're not using him anymore for woodworking jobs. See how all high and mighty he gets when he can't feed his family."

If you wanted business, you had to be on good terms with the world you lived in. Much of Revelation can be read as a call to resist those economic forces that diminish Christian commitments. Nowhere is this more evident than the number of the Beast.

666 Is the Loneliest Number

We're to the part where fun with numbers gets a little nutty in our day, but it's important to get this right or you might find yourself seeing the Antichrist in every license plate or receipt you get from Starbucks. I got on the scales the other morning and my weight was 166.6. My wife looked at the scale and murmured, "Antichrist . . . figures." Okay, I'm making this last one up, but you get it, amiright? This kind of thing happens every day for some people.

Ah, the number of the beast. When you first heard or read the words of Revelation, what did the number 666 mean? Probably not what it meant for those who first read the text. Some scholars speculate, based on the *gematria*, a system of adding up the numerical values of letters in a word, that the number was that of a real person. In antiquity, letters of the alphabet had numerical values assigned to them. It was easy to determine the number if you had the name, hard to determine the name if all you had was the number. Some commentators argue that if you take the Hebrew form of *Neron Caesar*, it comes out to 666, and even the variant reading of the number to 616 works if the Latin form *Nero Caesar* is used. This is a far more reasonable suggestion than current speculation on the number offers.

THE ELDER

I'm guessing a reasonable suggestion isn't what the Rapture crew is looking for.

The number 666 has exerted an almost perverse fascination for hundreds of years. Besides Nero, there have been countless others who had the number of the beast: Mussolini, Roosevelt, Hitler, even Ronald Wilson Reagan, who, because he had three names of six letters each, was identified as the Antichrist by some (http://www.666truth .org. Go ahead, check it out; I'm not making this stuff up). Others read the mark of the beast as being the number of humankind instead of a specific person. For example, this line of interpretation infers that in the context of Revelation we find the number 7 often used to denote perfection or completeness. The vials, trumpets, and seals all are finished at seven. In this context, the claim goes, the number 6 three times over (666) falls one short of perfection. That which is almost messianic, almost complete, falls short.[7]

There's no doubt that the number of the beast has exercised many imaginations over the centuries, eliciting wild fantasies. Everything from social security numbers to zip codes and credit card numbers have been identified as the harbingers of the Antichrist who seeks to control the world through the economic order. Usually socialism has

---

When I was young, my minister preached a sermon against Christians using barcode scanners.

THE DEACON

---

been the culprit for dispensationalists, but this cloaks the potential of capitalism as a candidate for demonic sway. That connection has certainly been made in other Christian communities (#liberationtheology).

Against this backdrop of beasts we again meet one like the Son of Man, coming on the clouds (14:14), only this time he wields a sickle, with which he harvests the earth, a horrific image of blood and death. Rivers of blood flow as high as a horse's bridle for two hundred miles

(14:20). Passages like these call forth our repugnance and embarrassment. It's hard to reconcile our images of Christ, forgiving his enemies and teaching his followers to love theirs, with rivers of blood. It's even harder to imagine so many of Jesus' contemporary followers eagerly anticipating the genocidal wrath of God.

The slaughter here (and that yet to come) raises questions about what type of God we're dealing with in this apocalypse. For those wed to a more literal reading, God is an avenging monster at the end of days. This is how other religious apocalypses unfold when destruction of all existing order ushers in a new age. Reading this text, we wonder if it's even possible for humankind to create a vision of God where love overcomes all that opposes it. Revelation stands as testimony to the difficulty of that vision taking root within us. For many, a vision of God where love overcomes evil makes a mockery of justice. We stand at the edge of mystery as we peer into Revelation's abyss.

As the recurring judgments continue to pour out in following chapters, we find the kings of the world assembling for battle on the great day of the Lord at Armageddon. In this moment the earth experiences such torments as rivers drying up, scorching sun, and people's tongues swollen and seared with intense heat—you know, like summer in North Carolina. There will be massive death and earthquakes unlike any ever experienced (think of the summer blockbuster, *San Andreas*).

This language of war and destruction wrenches us from the soft pathos of our liberal complacency, pulling us deeper into the chaos that millions of people face every day. There are those who are at the mercy of rulers who care nothing about them, leaders who desire only

If Dwayne Johnson played Jesus in the movie he could yell, "Finally the Christ has come back to earth." #SmellWhatTheChristIsCooking

THE ACOLYTE

to feather their own nests, and prophets who connive to buttress these deceivers with transcendent legitimation, claiming that their efforts at securing power are motivated by the desire to do God's will. How shall we sing the Lord's song in this peculiar Babylon?

The Late Great Babylon

Following the pouring out of the seven bowls of wrath we enter into the final moments of Rome, with one of the most compelling (and for contemporary readers one of the most misogynist) scenes in John's Revelation, the picture of the great whore of Babylon:

> Then one of the seven angels who had the seven bowls came and said to me, "Come, I will show you the judgment of the great whore who is seated on many waters, with whom the kings of the earth have committed fornication, and with the wine of whose fornication the inhabitants of the earth have become drunk." So he carried me away in the spirit into a wilderness, and I saw a woman sitting on a scarlet beast that was full of blasphemous names, and it had seven heads and ten horns. The

woman was clothed in purple and scarlet, and adorned with gold and jewels and pearls, holding in her hand a golden cup full of abominations and the impurities of her fornication; and on her fore-head was written a name, a mystery: "Babylon the great, mother of whores and of earth's abomina-tions." And I saw the woman was drunk with the blood of the saints and the blood of the witnesses to Jesus. (Revelation 17:1–6)

We find echoes of this figure in Ezekiel's condemna-tion of Tyre, a proud city, flush with gold and containing every kind of precious stone, but whose prosperity will end in destruction (Ezekiel 27–28). The whore represents a polar opposite to the previous 144,000 virgins who "have not defiled themselves with women" (Revelation 14:1–4). The treatment of this woman offends us with its blatant misogyny and we struggle with John's language, but con-temporary feminist scholars offer sharp and insightful commentary on the image of the whore.[8]

What follows after the metaphorical image of the whore is one of the few places in Revelation where the angelic messenger interprets what the vision means. Con-trary to the woman pursued by the dragon, the woman sit-ting on the scarlet beast full of blasphemous names reflects the system upon which the world rests. She is by appear-ance an alluring spectacle, clothed in jewels and beautiful clothes. She intoxicates the world, and offers the tempta-tion not just of sexual pleasure, but shopping malls.

She sits on seven mountains and no reader of this would have mistaken seven mountains for anything other than Rome, the city of seven hills (contemporary readers might be thrown by the fact that Lynchburg, Virginia, home of the late Jerry Falwell and stronghold of American dispensational fundamentalism, is also called the city of seven hills, but they shouldn't draw the same conclusions ancient readers did). Rome is Babylon, a place of exile, servitude, and alienation where we're cut off from home. The entire book of Revelation can be read as the unveiling of forces and pressures that call for Christians to compromise with a consuming power that demands obedience and allegiance. Later, when Christianity decided to take Rome up on its offer—we'll stop killing you if you agree to become a part of the empire—Rome starts to look somewhat different than an alluring, but toxic temptation. But that's a story for another day.

Perhaps conservatives misread Revelation and liberals avoid it because we just aren't

THE BISHOP

comfortable with the challenge it could pose to our blind nationalism.

The angel proceeds to tell an astonished John about multitudes of kings who have come, fallen, not yet come, who come for a little while, but they all have this in common—waging war on the Lamb. These kings give authority and power to the beast, making war on the Lamb, but the Lamb will overcome them. Eventually, no matter how many support the woman, how many she is responsible for, the kings and beast conspire against her, to make her desolate and naked. The beast turns against itself. We can assume that John was confronting the world of his day, but contemporary dispensational interpreters identify these figures with plenty of candidates in our time.

While speculation concerning horns, heads, and numbers has captivated generations, we may ask what importance any of this has to us today? If we grasp that Babylon not only was, but is, we find fruitful space for reflection. All that Babylon represents never truly dies; it only manifests itself in different ways. This is often hard for us to comprehend. As people of faith we may see the world as the good creation of God, enjoy the gifts of food, drink, and friends with gratitude, marvel at the creativity of our artists, and be blessed with a life that the kings of old would have envied. Doesn't God want us to have nice things?

Prophetic faith, however, questions the orders that shape our lives. It asks how the oppression of others secures our prosperity. Discerning faith ponders the invisible costs we don't see of how we live and confronts us about our collusion with Babylon. These are uneasy concerns to raise in the reading of an ancient text, but if we're to offer an alternative reading to the dispensationalist's model then we should bring apocalyptic texts into conversation with our time.

By the Shopping Malls of Babylon, We Hung Up Our Harps

One of the most compelling parts of John's apocalypse is the fall of Babylon. When Babylon falls, luxury and consumption are over, the kings and merchants of the earth, who have built systems of economic oppression to enrich themselves, wail at Babylon's demise: "And the merchants of the earth weep and mourn for her, since no one buys their cargo anymore, cargo of gold, silver . . . fine linen . . . spice, incense, myrrh . . . horses and chariots, slaves—and human lives" (Revelation 18:11–13).

And human lives. Let that sink in for a minute. #OccupyBabylon

This is followed by more woes: "The merchants of these wares, who gained wealth from her, will stand far off, in fear of her torment, weeping and mourning aloud . . . and all the shipmasters and seafarers, sailors and all whose trade is on the sea, stood far off and cried out as they saw the smoke of her burning, 'What city was like that great city?'" (Revelation 18:17). As the weeping and mourning over lost economic power continue, those who participated in this system and did not consider the price of their allegiance lose their world, and in the process, their souls.

I am guessing Christmas will look a bit different post-Babylon.

THE ELDER

When modern folk read this, we find ourselves confused. We're obsessed with trade; we build cities, celebrate artists, merchants, and athletes. We've even combined Nike (#justdoit) with commerce—to the victor go the spoils. We enjoy our minstrels and artisans; they make life worthwhile. And yet, there is rejoicing in heaven at the end of Babylon's music (19:1–6), though there's no more Nickelback so the news is not all bad. Still, God is such a

---

THE ACOLYTE

Nickelback is the Gen-X fannypack.

---

buzzkill sometimes. Upon closer inspection we discover that Babylon is not only the center of art and commerce, it's a place where humans are mistreated and oppressed, made to serve a system that cares nothing for them. Babylon is where humans are traded and enslaved, considered useful not because they are created in God's image, but only for the ways in which they can enrich Babylon itself. It's sobering to realize that in John's version of things, commerce and cultural activities represent a type of sorcery (18:23). Those enamored with free market capitalism will find no divine comfort in these passages, for the merchants of the earth suffer the stunning revelation that even commerce is never neutral, no matter how deeply we attempt to hide that fact. In God's reign, productivity is not seen as the measure of our worth. Heresy indeed.

For those who were at the mercy of a rapacious and narcissistic social order, whose existence in the world was to serve and attend to the pleasures and entertainment of others, the destruction of Babylon is freedom. Babylon is more like the society in *The Hunger Games* books and movies. In that world, all wealth flows from the periphery to the center; people are pitted against one another for the entertainment of a hollow elite; artificial sentiment is stoked by appeal to voyeuristic probing of strangers' lives; and human sacrifice is the price of order and peace. The collapse of that order means liberation to all those who do not share in its wealth. The irony is that those of us cheering on Katniss Everdeen in theaters actually belong to the group who can afford the movie ticket; we're the ones who live in the Capitol.

These haunting laments of merchants and rulers find answer in a new song, "the roar of a great multitude in heaven shouting, Hallelujah! Salvation and glory and power belong to our God" (Revelation 19:1). This is a jarring contrast. Our ability to identify with the cacophony of voices in Revelation varies depending on our circumstances. What might give us pause is an honest appraisal of which song we'll be singing at the last day. You can mourn with Babylon, or you can sing in heaven, but you can't do both.

It is with this that Revelation approaches its final act—the return of Christ, the binding of Satan, and the onset of the millennium, the thousand-year reign of God. After this thousand-year period of peace, however, Satan is inexplicably released from captivity to torment the earth yet again, leading to the really last battle—let's call this one Harmageddon—and then the judgment, the appearance of the new heaven and the new earth, culminating in the New Jerusalem.

These are the images that have shaped not just the Christian church, but Western civilization. While there may have been some who took these visions literally, John used metaphors to write a theology of resistance and hope. In anticipating Christ's return, early Christians found, just like Daniel, hope that the suffering of their lives would be redeemed by forces more powerful than the ones they endured; Revelation proclaimed that God had not abandoned them.

This millennial hope was not unique to Christianity; it existed in other Jewish texts like 2 Baruch where one of the material aspects of the new age is found in increased fruitfulness of the earth, where, "one vine will be a thousand branches and one branch will produce a thousand clusters." This is the promise of all apocalypses—the restoration of the entire earth to what it's supposed to be. In this way we could actually read the book of Revelation as the last great Jewish apocalypse.

Many in the early church anticipated the return of Christ in their day. They would be the ones to usher in the new age and welcome Christ when he came to rule the earth. But, as time passed and the first communities of Jesus' followers didn't experience their Lord's return, the landscape shifted a bit. In the face of disappointment, when the future becomes more opaque, how does one wait? Caught between the already of Christ's death and resurrection, a moment that changes the entire world, and the not yet of Christ's delay, how does the church wait? The answer is mixed, but we either wait in the hope that our future is found in our present, or we wait in anxiety for that destructive day of the Lord when all will be swept away. These are the paths people of faith have walked for millennia—with mixed results, as we shall see.

The Road to Where We Are

*All society, everywhere, with its politics, its phi-
losophy, and its religion, is in a perturbed condi-
tion. . . . The stream of earthly things is overflowing
its old banks, and spreading out in every direction,
in wild, disordered, ungovernable, and overwhelming volume. Old systems and modes of thought and
belief, which have stood for ages, are everywhere tot-
tering. . . . That 'the world to come' is . . . a vast
improvement upon the present scheme of things, will
be inferred on all hands without argument.*

The Reverend Joseph Seiss,
The Last Times, 1856

Rayford Steele, pilot for Pan-Continental Airlines, is
flying to London, anticipating a weekend of fun with
his senior flight attendant, Hattie Durham. Rayford's
wife, Irene, remains back home, presumably praying for
her wayward husband. Out over the Atlantic Ocean an
agitated Hattie informs Rayford that several dozen people

have suddenly disappeared from the plane, their clothes crumpled in the seats. The Rapture has struck, and after Rayford manages to land his plane in chaotic conditions, he returns home to find his daughter, Chloe, still on earth, but Irene and their son Raymie were taken by the Rapture. Thus begins the most recent version of the *Left Behind* saga. If you think you've lived through this nightmare before, you're right, only the last time it was Kirk Cameron as Rayford Steele. Apparently apocalypse porn has a half-life, destined to reappear every time geopolitical alignments change (note to self: develop new end times script with Russia, Syria, Iran, and ISIS as antagonists). I wonder if the people who make these movies are going to be among those weeping merchants when Babylon falls. The path from the powerful metaphorical images of Revelation to the kitschy but popular world of Christian Rapture fiction has been circuitous, but in this chapter I want to mark a bit of the trail for you.

I mentioned earlier that the book of Revelation was widely disputed for inclusion in the canon, the boundaries of which weren't established until the fifth century. Some scholars lay the hesitation about Revelation at the feet of Montanus, a man given to prophetic fervor, who preached in the second century CE that the New Jerusalem would descend from the clouds and land in the city of Phrygia. The church rejected Montanus's teachings, but his penchant for setting dates made folks skittish about millennialists. Even after Revelation was accorded the status of Christian Scripture, Greek theologians downplayed its apocalyptic themes and today it's still not used in Eastern Orthodox Divine Liturgy.

> If Bishops held a vote today to keep Revelation out of the canon I imagine it would pass.

THE BISHOP

Luther held the book in great suspicion, which is understandable given the role that Revelation played in stoking the Peasant's Revolt. Revelation's use to justify violent revolution has meant it can be like the neglected stepbrother we ignore until he wants to start a human petting zoo—it's harmless until it falls into the wrong hands (#DavidKoresh, #MosesDavid).

Apocalypse: The Early Days

In the first three centuries of Christianity, interpreters of Revelation reflected the social concerns of their time. During moments of increased persecution and social upheaval, the more apocalyptic elements were emphasized; in times of relative peace, readers found their own day a suitable candidate for the millennium. Though millenarian types like Montanus were the exception, apocalyptic expectations were still found in such second- and third-century writers as Justin, Irenaeus, Cyprian, Tertullian, and Hippolytus. At the end of the third century and leading into the fourth, when Diocletian was roasting Christians on his gridirons (can you ever look at a football field the same after knowing that?), Revelation acquired a fresh urgency among those who tied Rome's persecutions to the text.

Diocletian's persecution eventually burned out, but in its embers one of Christianity's more pivotal moments flared up, Constantine's desire to incorporate Christianity into the empire.

When the church's fortunes changed due to the Edict of Milan in 313, a universal decree of religious toleration issued by Constantine and Licinius, the edges of the church's apocalyptic interpretation softened. When the empire has you wrapped in animal skins and tossed into an arena full of lions it's easy to cast the emperor as the Antichrist, but when the emperor becomes the church's BFF what do you do? Few of the bishops who met at Nicaea in 325 to work out doctrine wanted to connect Constantine to the Antichrist—after all, he was paying their travel stipends, not to mention that he was probably plying them with excellent wine and delicacies ("Some more wolves' nipples chips, Arius?"). And, of course, there was that whole ending of persecution ("What have the bloody Romans ever done for us?"). Still, this being humankind and all, stability was an elusive prize in succeeding centuries. Even after Christianity's inclusion into the Roman Empire, there were moments of social and political chaos when apocalyptic ideas found expression in the familiar images, timelines, and metaphors of Revelation.

Sulpicius Severus (d. 420 CE), writing during a time when Rome was experiencing pressure from the barbarians, composed a history of the world that narrated end times scenarios no less fanciful than the *Left Behind* books. One of the most interesting aspects of his interpretation is the lingering belief that the Emperor Nero was somehow still alive. The story was that Nero—whose death had never been certified—was being kept alive until the end of time when he would return to power and rule with the Antichrist, who would rebuild the temple in Jerusalem, and fulfill all the biblical prophecy. It does make me wonder how many Nero sightings there were over the centuries. ("No, I heard he's on Sicily, a friend of mine swore he saw him playing dice in one of the casinos. Yeah, the toga was a little tight, but the sideburns gave him right away.") Sulpicius' master, Martin of Tours, even speculated that the Antichrist had been born in their time and walked among them.[1]

One North African writer, Tyconius (d. 400 CE), proposed that the millennial reign had already begun with Christ's first coming. Thus, the thousand-year reign was not in the future; it was present reality. He connected the binding of Satan by Jesus in Matthew 12:29 with the passage in Revelation where Satan was bound (Revelation 20:2). Since Jesus bound Satan, he reasoned, we must be in the millennial reign of God, though the release of Satan in Revelation implied we must always be alert for the presence of evil.

Jerome (d. 420 CE) thought Revelation might be referring to actual future persons and events, but even so, the allegorical and spiritual interpretations were more important. The shock of Rome's impending fall in 410 CE, however, darkened his mood. Jerome was not the only one who felt gloomy about the passing away of Rome; the pagans distressed by Rome's fading glory were so annoyed by it that they blamed the Christians for the demise. If the worship of their deities had not been deserted in favor of the Christian God, the pagans argued, the pagan gods may not have given over Rome to the barbarians.

It was Augustine's response to this pagan challenge that shaped centuries of Christian eschatological and political thought. In *The City of God* he opposed speculations as to when the world would end, contending that the thousand-year millennium was a way of speaking about time as a totality of history (18.53; 20.7). Augustine rejected a literal messianic reign in favor of the idea that the cross and resurrection were the first fruits of the new age, and the rule of the saints with Christ was the manifestation of Christ's presence in the church.

Augustine avoided reading current events in Rome or Hippo through an apocalyptic lens, even though in the early part of the fifth century a mood of panic swept through the Mediterranean world. Many people pointed to natural disasters like droughts, earthquakes, and eclipses as dire events that heralded the end of the world. Many of these anxious souls wrote to Augustine asking if the end was near.[2] Augustine responded to these fears with a tract, *On the End of the World*, where he counseled that we should wait with patience and love for the Lord's return and not calculate the date or speculate on the signs. He claimed that the three attitudes to take regarding Christ's return are: 1) that you can expect it soon, but in the process risk damaging your own or your neighbor's faith if it doesn't happen; 2) you can suppose it will be long delayed, and so train yourself in patience and be happily surprised if it occurs sooner than expected; or 3) you can simply be agnostic as Augustine is when he writes, "The one who admits that he or she does not know which of these expectations is true hopes for the one, is resigned to the other, and is wrong in neither of them."[3] If we paid as much attention to his eschatology as we do to his teachings on sex and original sin, the world might look a lot different. Just saying.

It's in Augustine's rejection of a literal millennialism in place of a more nuanced understanding of history that his contribution to eschatology shifts the focus. Not speculative, not predictive, his history oscillates between two poles—Rome and Jerusalem. These two entities, prominently featured in Revelation, allow Augustine to read a corporate reality into the struggle of Christ and the world. The Beast is not an individual, but the communities who oppose God's people. There is an ongoing tension between these two orders that creates the animating energies and powers made visible in the state and church. Augustine's interpretation of sacred and secular history profoundly influenced all future Christian eschatology. In his hands the apocalyptic motif became "part of the everyday fabric of Christian life and belief, and to that extent reinforced eschatological awareness by embedding it in liturgy and preaching."[4]

Medieval Apocalypse: Working Out the Prototypes

Even though Augustine helped shift the church's gaze, the attraction of millenarian imagination remained, in no small part because the medieval world lived with plagues, destruction, and continual uncertainty—all candidates for apocalyptic speculation. What Augustine took away, however, one of the most famous interpreters of apocalyptic texts, Joachim of Fiore (1135–1202), brought back with his revival of millenarian ideas. In a precursor to modern dispensationalism, Fiore divided history into three interlocking parts, corresponding to the three persons of the Trinity: the period of the Father, which was creation to the coming of Christ; the period of the Son, which began earlier than Jesus, but reached fullness with Christ; and the period of the Spirit, which was marked by the rise of monastic orders and the reforms of Saint Benedict.

Internationally known for his schemes, Joachim took the images of Revelation and figured out who the opponents of Christianity were, identifying one of the heads of the beast in Revelation with his contemporary, Saladin, the Muslim leader (#everythingoldisnewagain). He was not alone in this speculation as some of his contemporaries identified Emperor Frederick II with one of the heads of the beast of Revelation, whereupon Frederick's supporters fired back that the numerical value of Pope Innocent IV's name and title added up to 666. Given this illustrious history, I suppose it's only a matter of time before charges of being the Antichrist start showing up in our political discourse. Oh, wait . . . http://www.inquisitr .com/1846796/obama-is-not-the-antichrist-hes-the -seventh-king-before-the-antichrist-newspaper-issues -correction/, which brings us to . . . wait for it . . . http:// www.cogwriter.com/hillary-clinton-prophecy-antichrist .htm. See, this craziness is not new with us, and it won't stop when we're gone.

It wasn't just Joachim, however, who speculated on the end times—the medieval period was a fertile field for plowing the apocalyptic ground. From peasants to kings, the fields of France to the hallowed halls of Oxford and Cambridge, and even to Jerusalem, a strong sense of apocalyptic urgency swept through European society, launching crusades and inspiring monastic orders like the

Franciscans. The dark shadow of this was cast by those who identified Jews and Muslims—two communities that Christianity has happily persecuted—as aligned with the demonic forces of the Antichrist. Revelation in the hands of fear mongers often leads to horrible carnage.

Throughout history apocalyptic rhetoric has infused political struggles between popes and emperors, clergy and laypeople, rulers and subjects. Antichrists have been readily identified, and this rhetoric has mobilized multitudes to violence and destruction. This has especially been the case in moments of social transitions when survival seemed most precarious. Everywhere that apocalypses have found space in the cultural imagination, the results have been the tendency to define events based on the images found in books like Revelation.

Could you imagine the foreign policy if Revelation read more like an episode Care Bears?

THE DEACON

For instance, in the medieval period the Antichrist acquired a type of resumé. It was believed he would be a Jew from the tribe of Dan and that he would be born in Babylon of human parents. Signs surrounding the Antichrist's appearance often reflected the perceived decadence of the age. This identification of the Antichrist with social anxiety allowed for the demonization of enemies, most often heretics and Jews, but also Muslims and Turks.

The Antichrist was a pliable figure, easily molded into whatever shape your enemy looked like.

This mutability stretched along a continuum of definition. Sometimes the Antichrist was portrayed as a corporate entity, as in Rome; at other times the Antichrist was portrayed as an individual, often the pope or Muslim rulers. Individualized, he became the figure who would rebuild the temple or make a covenant with Jews to give them Jerusalem.[5] As the medieval period gave rise to the Renaissance and Reformation, the song remained the same. Luther called both the pope and the revolutionary Thomas Müntzer, the Antichrist.

If the popes of Joachim's time encouraged his visions because it served their interests in mobilizing for the crusades, by the time the peasants of Europe had lit multitudes of human torches, many in the church understood the danger in fomenting apocalyptic fantasies. The war of the saints on the Antichrist and his minions, ending in a flowing river of blood up to a horse's bridle, was supposed to happen in the valley of Megiddo, not the Rhine Valley.

Apocalypse: The New World

Different forms of eschatology colored the old world, but some Christians, seeing Europe more like Babylon, turned their attention to a Promised Land across the Atlantic Red Sea and set out for their fresh New Jerusalem. From the beginning America held the promise of a city on the hill, a light to the Gentiles, and the redeemer nation for the rest of the world. This meant that in the American experience the end of the world was transformed into a postmillennial understanding of history where the gradual improvement of the world unfolded according to rational laws and faith in orderly progression.

Throughout the early history of America, millennial hopes were translated to the new situation. Biblical allusions to prophecy suggesting America's importance in God's plans were thick in sermons and pamphlets, some of which proclaimed the American experiment as the place where God's reign on earth would commence. Cotton Mather had no problem setting dates, which he placed variously at 1697, 1716, and 1736. God's millennial kingdom seemed ever more present on earth as it was in heaven.[6] Mather stood in a long tradition of interest in the end times, and was one of the first in a long line of American theologians to read the history of God's timeline with American lenses.

Cotton Mather
also enjoyed witch
hunting. A clear sign of
levelheaded thinking.

THE ELDER

Okay, so just checking in, is all this history making you sleepy? Bored? We're just about at the really interesting part, but I wanted to show you that this whole apocalyptic craziness has been going on a long time. However, we have to go down the road a bit more to find out why Nicolas Cage follows Kirk Cameron in a role neither of them should've played (although I'm sure when you have mouths to feed, a guy's gotta do what a guy's gotta do, right Nicolas?).

Although Enlightenment-oriented preachers and teachers embraced the biblical criticism coming from Europe, evangelicals in America weren't having any of that. In fact, many of them would veer off in a direction—fundamentalism—that would hook up with dispensationalism to spawn the great American heresy. America has always been fertile ground for all types of innovation (#SteveJobs), but we can be a bit perplexed at times. The premillennial interpretation tended toward pessimism about us, despairing of our ability to follow God. Evangelical Christians often found a more congenial home in the story of Noah, where human degradation and sinfulness compelled God to destroy the earth. In America this pessimism found itself at odds with the optimism that drove this country. (Or maybe it was manifest destiny that drove the country. Sometimes this is confusing.)

Apocalypticism found a home in America among communities that didn't share the liberal, triumphant view that America was God's city upon a hill, established as a beacon for the world. Shakers, Mormons, the Amish and Mennonites, the followers of John Humphrey Noyes in the Oneida community, as well as many other communities, chose separation from the wicked and fallen world of their brethren. Given the number of emotional upheavals that pulsated through areas such as the burned-over district in western upstate New York, it was no surprise that many of the most well-known apocalyptic voices hailed from there.

It would be a devout, self-taught Baptist biblical scholar, however, who captured attention with his end times speculation in the middle of the nineteenth century. William Miller, also from the burned-over district of upstate New York, grew intrigued by the book of Daniel. Like thousands before him, he jumped down the rabbit hole of biblical numbers and focused on Daniel 8:14, which reads: "Unto two thousand and three hundred days; then shall the sanctuary be cleansed." From such small beginnings came interesting results. Using methods created solely from his imagination, he calculated from this and other verses that the return of Christ would occur around the year 1843.

Thousands found his preaching and teaching compelling and through huge tent rallies and services they came into contact with mass-produced tracts and periodicals containing fascinating colorful charts and apocalyptic imagery of lions, bears, and dragons. A Millerite movement grew in the northern tier of the country, eagerly anticipating the end of the world. When 1843 came and went, some grew disillusioned, but others were willing to double down. Eventually a precise date was established, October 22, 1844. When that day came and went the movement collapsed overnight, but all was not lost. After the "Great Disappointment," the anticipation it generated was not easily put to rest as searching for the apocalypse became, like baseball, one of America's great pastimes.[7] For example, from the ashes of this failure arose the Seventh Day Adventist movement. Miller had established organizational and publicity mechanisms that would provide a model for those to come, most notably those who followed the teachings of an Irish Christian by the name of John Nelson Darby.

What a Long Strange Trip—John Nelson Darby and the Plymouth Brethren

Great Britain also had those like Edward Irving and Henry Drummond who preached apocalypticism, often with a keen interest in the history of the Jews and their restoration to the Promised Land as a sign of the last days. This new apocalyptic interest in the United Kingdom grabbed the attention of a young priest, John Nelson Darby, who was recovering from a serious leg injury in 1827. Ordained in the (Protestant) Church of Ireland in 1825, Darby later rejected his ordination, thereby following a pattern of others who could not find satisfaction in traditional forms of Christianity. He endured a period of anxiety that led to a religious experience that he testified united him with Christ in heaven. After this experience he joined a group of dissenters who split in two, with Darby becoming the leader of the Plymouth Brethren. If we want to trace the roots of American fundamentalism and its understanding of the end times, the major path takes us back to Darby and his system of dispensationalism.

Following in the steps of Joachim of Fiore, Darby taught that God had divided up human history—from the Garden of Eden to the millennial kingdom found in the book of Revelation—into periods of time or *dispensations*. We read previously that in each of these dispensations the means of salvation would be different; God's action with humans depended on the epoch. The time of Adam and Eve differed from the time of Noah, which differed from

the time of Abraham and so on. When Darby was working this out he decided that the Age of the Church began
with the time of the apostles and continues on into the
present day. In this scheme, one cycle of prophesied events
ends with Jesus' resurrection and God's clock doesn't start
ticking again until the last week of Daniel's seventy weeks
when the Rapture strikes, kicking off the last seven years
so colorfully fictionalized in numerous prophecy novels.

This outline works
better with pictures and
a chart.

THE DEACON

After the believers have risen to meet Christ, leaving
their clothes on Rayford Steele's airplane, the floors of
shopping malls, and the driver's side of crashed cars, the
final sequence of earth's history commences, a horrific
seven-year period where the Antichrist and apostate
church reign, leading to the battle of Armageddon and the
"true" return of Jesus. Like William Miller, Darby looked
to the book of Daniel for this inspiration. Using the reference to "seventy weeks" in Daniel 9:22–27, Darby claimed
that the seventy weeks were actually seventy "sevens" or
490 years. In his scheme the first sixty-nine weeks of this
period have already occurred, but with Christ's death God
pushed the pause button and now we wait on the seventi-
eth week, the seven-year period of terror marking the end
of the church age. One wonders how many pints of Guinness were consumed before this revelation hit Darby.

Unfair shot? Maybe so, but it's so hard to blame the Bible for this whole thing.

THE ELDER

Guinness has a very low ABV. He sounds more like an Imperial Bourbon Barrel Aged Stout kind of guy.

Using Daniel's symbolic times for the end of Antiochus's reign as literal prophecies of the end of the world, Darby believed that after the Rapture the Antichrist would consolidate power and set up his reign in the middle of this last "week," which is three-and-a-half years, or forty-two months. Combining these numbers with those in Revelation, Darby preached that the Antichrist would take power at the midpoint of the last seven-year period. At the end of the seven years Christ and the saints return to earth to initiate divine genocide.

Since the same timelines were in Daniel and Revelation, Darby assumed they were addressing the same thing: the end of the world. Familiarity with apocalyptic literature might have clued Darby in on the fact that these are not numbers to take literally, but millions today follow Darby's interpretations, especially the *Left Behind* books and movies. Of course, this interpretation believes that the millennium is a literal thousand-year reign of Christ. The thought that the millennium may be a symbolic metaphor to get at something less literal than days or months is not an option for dispensationalists.

Darby's system had massive theological implications. The Rapture of an invisible church meant that all public and institutional forms of the church such as mainline denominations were aligned with Babylon and thus beyond redemption. This not only justified the special status of the Plymouth Brethren, but all those who condemn the evils of the denominational churches. At the end of the world, the true believers, like Irene Steele and others who vanished, will be revealed as the true chosen ones. All those compromisers and lukewarm believers like New Hope Village's visitation minister, Bruce Barnes and poor, poor Patty Jo Meyers, will have to suffer the consequences of their unbelief.

Creating Fundamentalism: C. I. Scofield and the Scofield Reference Bible

While meeting with some success in the United Kingdom, Darby's system would really flourish in God's new chosen nation. The planting of his ideas in the fertile ground of American soil, a nation unencumbered with the historical perspective of Europe, yielded the greatest crop of believers in dispensationalism. Some of this was due to Darby's indefatigable energy in coming to America and spreading his gospel, but the majority of credit should go to the accomplishments of a Tennessee farmer and Civil War veteran named Cyrus Ingerson Scofield. He was a colorful character, whose life before conversion was marked by excessive drinking, marital problems, and accusations of theft and forgery. I must emphasize here that we should not be too quick to judge (#glasshouses, #stones). He experienced a dramatic conversion in jail and soon came under the influence of James H. Brookes, an ardent believer in Darby and his dispensational ideas.

Scofield's greatest achievement was the *Scofield Reference Bible*, published by Oxford University Press in 1909. In a fortuitous moment of timing, some American evangelicals were responding to the challenges of modernity by publishing the first of what would become known as *The Fundamentals*, a series of writings that sought to define the doctrines of what "true" Christianity should look like. These writings shaped fundamentalist beliefs and continue to do so. Scofield's Bible commentary and *The Fundamentals* joined together to create the contours of a distinctly American premillennial fundamentalism. Just as the first works of *The Fundamentals* were published, Scofield introduced millions to the world of the Rapture, the Great Tribulation, fascinating charts, and premillennialism, not to mention predictions of the Jews returning to Israel and Russia as the Gog of the Bible. From the time Scofield's Bible was published, it became the definitive source for understanding all things dispensationalist. Because of the way that Scofield embedded his commentary within the text of the Bible, some people even accepted his exegesis as divinely inspired. The lines between interpretation and scripture were blurred in many people's minds. The influence of this book cannot be underestimated. Thousands of graduates, among them Hal Lindsey, of fundamentalist and dispensational schools like the former Dallas Bible College, now Dallas Theological Seminary, have been preaching and teaching their congregations about the return of Christ using interpretations found in Scofield.

Scofield reflected the pessimism of those who see little goodness in humankind. Human nature is fallen, without redemptive merit outside the sacrifice of Christ, and bound for destruction. His work teems with a deep suspicion about humans and their institutions, including the church, but it was widely appreciated by growing numbers of fundamentalists, not the least because Scofield masterfully interpreted scripture in a way that was accessible to laypeople and spoke to them. The *Scofield Reference Bible* railed against many of the concerns that modernity posed for conservative Christians.

During the late nineteenth century when various prophecy conferences were held, liberal theology, with its affirmation of Darwin, science, and biblical criticism could be dismissed as part of the "signs of the times." Liberals

---

"Liberal" is used very broadly among dispensationalists. My youth minister warned us about CS Lewis and NT Wright . . .

THE DEACON

---

opposed the truth because they were heretics prophesied about in the Bible. In fact, modern theology was just a predicted part of the world's apostasy away from God, a sure signal that the end was close, and as it was then, so it remains. This is the power of apocalyptic thinking—all the social changes that perplex believers, the course of global events, can be pressed into service to show how close we are to the end of all things. The world's refusal to accept this "truth" only serves as evidence that the believer is right.

In the late nineteenth and early twentieth century, the liberal idea of progress was a heresy to be fought in the face of Jesus' soon returning (in fairness, fundamentalists weren't the only ones casting doubt, *cough*, Karl Barth, *cough*, on the liberal slogan that "in every day, and in every way, we're getting better and better"). Christ was coming at any moment, not after a long period of human progress. These ideas heavily influenced the direction of American Christianity, especially in its fundamentalist and evangelical expressions. Dispensational premillennialism became a part of the most famous evangelical preachers' repertoire. Dwight Moody, Billy Sunday, R. A. Torrey, and many more spread the gospel of Christ's imminent return. Networks of schools and conferences blossomed on the American landscape to proclaim the message that Jesus was coming back *any minute*.

One of Darby and Scofield's most compelling and innovative claims was the idea of the Rapture. Popularized by charts, cartoons, images, and pictures of people ascending into the sky to meet Jesus, the Rapture drives contemporary apocalyptic narrative. We even see it on bumper stickers: "Warning: car will be driverless in case of Rapture." A friend gave me a bumper sticker I have on my office door that reads, "Come the Rapture, can I have your car?"

The Rapture was never really a part of Christian tradition, but Darby found justification for it in the passage we read earlier, 1 Thessalonians 4:15–17. Darby taught that this moment could happen in the twinkling of an eye, and this is the way it's been portrayed and popularized in American culture. The Rapture is no longer just a theological interpretation; in the minds of millions the Rapture is an eagerly awaited, or fearfully anticipated, event. The interesting (and perhaps terrifying) thing is that dispensationalism affects our culture more than we might realize, extending into the very halls of political power.

The avenue for this impact was paved in the nineteenth century through a group of radical evangelicals and their Bible conferences in the United States and Canada. Disillusioned by the mainstream traditions, an American proclivity where religion is concerned, they set up the Niagara Bible Conferences of 1875–1897, as well as speaking tours for Darby, who spent a total of six years in North America between the years 1862 and 1877. These events were wildly successful, drawing thousands of laypeople and ministers to hear the gospel of dispensationalism. Matthew Sutton makes the argument in his book, *American Apocalypse*, that premillennialism offered those on the margins of American society a way of leveling the field.[8] But, it wasn't just the poor who embraced the teachings; wealthy patrons often funded the conferences that helped establish dispensationalism as one of the distinguishing marks of American fundamentalist Christianity.

Outside of the Niagara conferences, one of the first major gatherings of dispensationalists was held in New York City in the fall of 1878 at the Church of the Holy Trinity. The meeting was intended to make sense of current events in the light of biblical prophecy. The attendees came from a vast array of denominations and this very ecumenism was seen as evidence that God was moving in the last days—and the logic preached at these meetings still holds sway today. Those who did not accept the teaching that Jesus was coming soon were not true believers, but liberals and modernists who had one foot in hell anyway. Once locked into this logic, it's hard to break through it.

This is one of the ways that systems of thought gain so much power over us: a particular type of logic or rationality is baked into the system so that when it's challenged the critique can be dismissed. The most powerful ideologies are the ones that are so tightly constructed they become "the truth" and no other perspective can challenge the system. Darby and Scofield were able to construct a system through

---

THE ELDER

Reminds me of trickle-down economics.

---

prooftexting scripture that made it seem so inherently logical it was the only viable interpretation of the end times.

American Apocalypse

Dispensationalism claimed to be a recovery effort, an attempt to retrieve what was forgotten. But in American society it also functioned as a tool of critique for all the ills that evangelical preachers believed corroded their world. It has served this function ever since, almost always working to critique liberalism as a sign of the last days and the need for a cleansing flood to renew American culture. Dispensationalism informed the views of millions of Americans about the nature of the state and what Christians owed to it. At the beginning of the twentieth century when the issue of how American Christians understood their cultural identity became a pressing issue, there was no unanimity among dispensationalists about how one should regard the government. World War I, however, forced dispensationalists to define their relationship to the state, and a good number, like the evangelist Billy Sunday, ardently embraced patriotism, even if God was getting ready to judge the country.

World War II also affected many dispensationalists, most of whom dropped their suspicion of Roosevelt's "socialist" government in favor of a robust response to Hitler's threat. The blending of nationalism, patriotism, and premillennialism made it easier after the war to enlist America on the side of the angels during the long postwar situation with Russia, but this patriotism stood in continual tension with the view of America that flourished in many prophecy books after World War II. In many of those works, America was a moral cesspool, allowing decadent society to corrupt the young, while the righteous suffered persecution for their faith (if you're not hearing this same theme now, it's because you're not paying attention). Conservative Christians in America only feel more embattled, persecuted, and closer to the end times as they watch their privileged place in society erode.

The list of end times degeneracy in America has been extensive over the last 150 years: Broadway, racial equality, women's rights, homosexuality (in fact, pretty much anything having to do with sex), even women clergy; all of these have been and still are candidates for signs of America's moral decay and impending judgment. Actually, anything having to do with women claiming their rights of full participation in society has been a sign of the last days.

Getting the right to vote in 1913 was seen as the work of demon-possessed women and a sign of the lawlessness predicted for the end times. Worries about the erosion of male authority in home, school, and church were voiced with the confidence that these things were reflective of the end of the age.[9]

At various times in this country, unions were seen as the work of the devil and the New Deal was a demonic attack on the godliness of free market capitalism. Socialism was the economic system of the Antichrist and capitalism the bulwark against it. But this only points out the ambiguity present in prophecy interpretation. Other evangelical preachers were so alienated from the world around them that they preached against capitalism as a sign of the decay of the world. Echoing the same themes we hear in our day, they railed against plutocracy, the wealth gap, and Wall Street, reading Revelation as a warning against all who would economically oppress the average person. If the evangelical community believed this today, America would be a far different country. This ambivalence concerning economic structures continues to the present day as some prophecy advocates like Hal Lindsey lean to the far right of the political spectrum, praising free market capitalism, while other prophecy writers believe that America's affluence is just another sign of end times corruption.

One of the most striking characteristics of the dispensational worldview has been the perennial suspicion of anything that smacks of global cooperation. When the League of Nations was formed in 1920, dispensational believers warned that any institution that worked for peace was a tool of Satan to enslave humankind. This suspicion of international

I have no reference point
for this type of thought.
I swear you are making
me scared of Christians!

THE ACOLYTE

cooperation extends to the present-day United Nations and
any other group that represents a global response to the challenges facing our world. Fear of the coming world system
among dispensationalists also characterizes their approach
to organizations of religious cooperation. According to the
dispensationalists of the early twentieth century, the Federal
Council of Churches was a nefarious attempt to corrupt society, as were its successors, the National Council of Churches
and the World Council of Churches. For Christians who are
immersed in premillennial dispensationalism, Satan in the
last days will bring the world's religions together for a great
apostasy. This is the meaning of the beast in Revelation 13,
who leads the world to worship the Antichrist. It goes without saying that multifaith efforts of any sort are viewed as
sure signs of Satan's work.

Cooperative efforts outside of organizations like the
National Alliance of Evangelicals (and even they're looked
at askance when they go rogue, like when they admitted
that maybe, just maybe, humans are responsible for climate change) are seen as signs of last-day apostasy. Perhaps this is because most popular prophecy "experts" exist
outside the halls of power where institutions like the
National Council of Churches are created and sustained.
Organizations founded by Christian liberals usually don't
engage with dispensationalists, who tend to become

defensive when challenged. We see the consequences of this belief every day on the American landscape.

THE ELDER

I'm not sure how to engage? I am pretty sure they consider Episcopalians non-Christians.

There's always been a type of quasi-religious sense about America and her destiny in dispensational accounts, but this was held in tension with the belief that American society was hopelessly fallen away from God. Between the battering of the country through the Civil War, the growing divide of rich and poor in the Gilded Age, the shock of world wars, and the struggles of the Great Depression, the once-bright future of America as God's new chosen nation faded. In the hands of dispensationalists, the America described after World War II found itself in the devil's clutches, descending with frightening rapidity into the pit of Satan's own moral decadence. How else to explain the sixties, disco, or frozen Margaritas?

THE BISHOP

I appreciate both.

Increasingly in the writings and speeches of men like John Walvoord, Pat Robertson, Jack van Impe, David Wilkerson, and Hal Lindsey, America was no longer the last best promise for the manifestation of God's reign on earth, rather—and this was especially true when a Democrat was president—it was more like Sodom and Gomorrah. This passive-aggressive approach to American

---

They weren't alone. Billy Graham once said God would have to apologize to Sodom and Gomorrah if He let America off the hook.

THE ELDER

---

culture still shows up in the *Left Behind* series and other books of biblical prophecy as secular humanists, college professors, and government bureaucrats are cast as stooges of evil (I'd totally go to see a band with that name). It's like the Axis of Evil, but different.

All of this points to the wide variety of responses that believers in the imminent end times have about American society. It's hard to understand fundamentalism and the most conservative forms of evangelicalism in America without the recognition of how significantly dispensationalism has affected society. The views of presidents, preachers, and laypeople have been shaped by dispensational ideas. It's almost a matter of pride in some dispensational circles that the learned teachers, philosophers, and intellectuals of our culture reject their ideas as preposterous.

Dispensationalism is the dominant perspective concerning the apocalyptic imaginary of American culture, and has created the false consciousness out of which millions of Americans look at the world. This has had enormous impact on American Christianity.

If this odd take on apocalyptic literature only affected a small part of America's population, we would have little to concern us, but dispensationalism is the lens through which millions of Americans interpret the fate and future of Israel. And this means that the connection between prophecy and Israel has striking implications for American foreign policy and our future in the Middle East. It's for this reason that dispensationalism is not just a harmless set of theological innovations that might amuse us, but a creator of reality that affects us all.

Jerusalem O Jerusalem

It is hoped that one day world Jewry will realize that Bible-believing, premillennialist Christians are Israel's best friends.

Tim LaHaye, *Coming Peace in the Middle East*

It took a Hitler to turn the Jews toward Palestine. It will take a greater Hitler to turn them to God.

Arthur Bloomfield, *How to Recognize the Antichrist*

In October of 1990 a group called the Temple Mount Faithful announced plans to lay a cornerstone during the Jewish holiday week of Sukkot for a future temple that would be rebuilt on the Temple Mount in Jerusalem. This attracted the attention of Palestinian Arabs who gathered to protect the honor of their sacred site, Al-Haram al-Sharif. The Palestinians, feeling embattled, pitched rocks at Jews praying at one of their most sacred

123

sites, the Western Wall. Israeli police initially responded to this provocation with restraint, falling back in the face of flying rocks. Later, however, they regrouped and raked the crowd of Palestinians with automatic weapons, leaving twenty-one dead and 125 wounded in their wake. Twenty-five years later the tensions between these two communities concerning the Temple Mount/Al-Haram al-Sharif have only exacerbated the social and political situation, threatening to plunge Israel into another Intifada.[1]

Theological beliefs affect the world; nowhere is this more apparent today than the State of Israel. And, of all the theological beliefs that potentially impact us, none are so deadly as those surrounding the constellation of ideas swirling around interpretations of biblical prophecy and the end of the world. The political and public policy concerns relating to Israel are profoundly influenced by groups of people from a diverse number of religious communities who see in Israel the fulfillment of prophecies made thousands of years ago. Like Shakespeare says, the past is always prologue.

If this is true, then we have to consider humankind's past and its use of violence to secure what was, and still is, considered sacred space. Those who have internalized apocalyptic rhetoric are most often in danger of unwittingly creating the very thing they hope for. This is especially true of those who believe that Christ's return can happen at any moment. For example, evangelical Christian leaders, encouraged by Israel's offers of free "familiarization" visits in the 1980s, were the vanguard of large numbers of dispensational Christian tourists who would come to Israel, tour the Holy Land, and leave aligned with the most right-wing elements in Israeli politics. Stoked by the belief that theirs is the last generation, these Christian tourists would be fed a narrative that matched their notions of Jesus' imminent return.[2]

When it comes to Israel and the Middle East, a case could certainly be made that the rise of Christian Zionism and the many preachers, teachers, groups, and websites dedicated to Christian Zionism's goals are emboldening forces in Israel that will lead to great chaos. When the *Left Behind* website says that the veil between the fiction of *Left Behind* and the reality of life in the Middle East is a thin one, this signals that they believe current events are part of the blueprint for the end of the world. This moves us from

---

I am guessing every youth group doesn't write letters to their congressman in support of funding the Israeli army?

THE DEACON

---

a bemused interest in prophecy to deadly serious struggling with how these beliefs can lead the world into destruction and violence. We face the question of accountability. Taking the apocalyptic proclivities of millions of people and feeding that beast with images of Manichaean showdowns between good and evil incites violence and hatred. How we deal with apocalyptic texts, the way they are taught, what they provoke in others, deserves closer examination. Feeding the idea that we're part of the divine plan for the end of the world makes us susceptible to those who would manipulate us to destructive action.

As we have seen, dispensationalists took their cues from the teachings of John Darby and Cyrus Scofield. This script placed Israel at the center of the world's drama and made certain assumptions about Israel's role in end times prophecy and the way the future unfolds. Darby drew a hard line between the church and Israel. He profoundly disconnected the people of Israel from the early followers of Jesus by misreading Paul. In his scheme the branch of the tree represented by Israel fell into unbelief, replaced by those who believed in the Jewish messiah, Jesus Christ. In Darby's interpretation, Israel disappears from the stage until the Rapture. The church age is like a "great parenthesis," marking time until the really important stuff kicks in after the Rapture takes place. Though Darby's exegesis makes about as much sense as the movie *Interstellar*, millions are swept up in the excitement that theirs is the last generation. The desire to be unique has spawned many monsters.

Can Christians Be Zionists?

THE ACOLYTE

I am anticipating an affirmative answer that has something to do with God saving some and killing more.

From Darby on, multitudes fixated on Israel and formed the foundation of what is known as Christian Zionism. In the nineteenth and early twentieth centuries these beliefs influenced a number of influential people in politics. Lord Anthony Ashley Cooper, the Earl of Shaftesbury, convinced the British government to open a consulate in Jerusalem, whose duties were to look after the interest of the Jews living in Palestine under the Ottoman Empire. William Blackstone, a Chicago businessman and prophecy writer, presented to President Benjamin Harrison "a memorandum urging U.S. support for a Jewish homeland in Palestine," partly in order to fulfill biblical prophecy. Even though they were not wild about the secular nature of Theodore Herzl's Zionism, they welcomed his movement as a step toward the fulfillment of biblical prophecy.[3] But it was the Balfour Declaration that had prophecy believers jumping in anticipation. Issued in 1917, the document called for "the establishment in Palestine of a national home for the Jewish people." Prophecy fans kept their eyes firmly focused on Israel, overlooking whatever atrocities may have occurred in the process of making Palestine into Israel.

Speculation about Israel's place in end times prophecy would go off the charts when one of the most important events anticipated by dispensationalists happened—on May 14, 1948, Israel was proclaimed a nation in Palestine. For dispensationalists this was not one moment among many in the flux of world history, it was biblical prophecy coming true. The linchpin to Darby's scheme—Israel— was put into place, so that the hinge of history could swing open for the final drama. Believers reminded their critics that Darby, Scofield, and many others had predicted this event, thus proving the truth of their interpretations.

Certainly dispensationalists like Hal Lindsey, Tim LaHaye, John Hagee, and countless others read into events surrounding Israel the fulfillment of prophecy. Lindsey called Israel "the fuse of Armageddon" and suggested that now, after having been taken to "God's woodshed" by Babylon and Rome—not to mention generations of Christians who persecuted and slaughtered Jews throughout Europe—God had restored Israel in order to start the clock ticking on the return of Jesus. (This theology, that God takes people to the "woodshed" for a genocidal beating, is probably behind the torture porn "hell house" creations that evangelicals throw up every Halloween to make the piss run down terrified teenagers' legs in some godforsaken cornfield somewhere. Jesus may love you, but God's wrath is guaranteed to give you a good adrenaline buzz when you see the hell prepared for you.)

THE DEACON

The first time I went to meet my future In-Laws they were in a production of "Heaven's Gates, Hell's Flames." He was playing Satan.

Stringing along scripture verses in his trademark way, Lindsey claimed that Israel's return to Palestine was the first of three major events, the other two being the repossession of Jerusalem and the rebuilding of a third temple.

Lindsey, drawing on Matthew's apocalypse, took a parable Jesus gave the disciples to spin his particular interpretation:

From the fig tree learn its lesson: as soon as its branch becomes tender and puts forth its leaves, you know that summer is near. So also, when you see all these things, you know that he is near, at the very gates. Truly I tell you, this generation will not pass away until all these things have taken place. Heaven and earth will pass away, but my words will not pass away. (Matthew 24:32–33)

In his distinctively creative way, Lindsey argues that Matthew was obviously addressing the restoration of the Jews to Palestine at the end of time. In his mind (and the millions who follow him), Israel was putting forth new leaves when the United Nations voted for a Jewish state in Palestine. This spin has become a crucial part of dispensationalism, but it was created out of whole cloth. The exegetical innovation involved in reading Jesus' parable of the fig tree as applying to our time is astonishing; in the dispensational world, however, this makes perfect sense.

I can't believe this nonsense has such a huge audience!

THE BISHOP

It's at this point that Lindsey wrote one of those predictions he is prone to make and which invariably disappear years later when things turn out differently than he anticipated. Taking the verse where Jesus says to the assembled disciples, "Truly I say to you, *this generation* will not pass away until all these things take place," Lindsey makes a stunning leap to argue that Jesus must have meant that the original hearers could not have been the generation Jesus had in mind:

> What generation? Obviously, in context, the generation that would see the signs—chief among them the rebirth of Israel. A generation in the Bible is something like forty years. If this is a correct deduction, then within forty years or so of 1948, all these things could take place. Many scholars who have studied Bible prophecy all their lives believe that this is so.[4]

The year 1988 must have been a bit of a bummer for those who put their faith in brother Hal. The Meh Disappointment. Lindsay is not alone in assigning contemporary importance to Israel. The website for *Left Behind* also sees Israel's importance in God's master plan: "Of the thirty or more signs of the end of time as we know it, which will culminate with the return of Christ to set up His 1,000-year reign on earth, none is more specific and convincing than the re-gathering of over one third of the world's Jews into the Land of Israel during the last century and the establishment of the State of Israel in 1948."[5]

1948—The Clock Starts Ticking

Those reading Lindsey, LaHaye, Hagee, and all the other prophecy purveyors are encouraged to believe they are on the cusp of something life-changing, but nowhere in the New Testament do we find what dispensationalists have created. Unlike Ryan Adams who takes Taylor Swift's *1989* and creates a work of genius, the clumsy hands of dispensationalists take the original text and destroy it. Most of the authors of New Testament texts were writing after the fall of Jerusalem in 70 CE, when Jewish political independence was impossible. Yet, mistaken as they were, they anticipated the return of Christ in their time without the necessity of a Jewish state, city, or temple. This extends to the book of Revelation, which clearly speaks of Christ's return, but nowhere is Israel as a state mentioned as a prerequisite: "No passage in the New Testament makes Jesus' return contingent on the re-establishment of a Jewish state."[6]

For dispensationalists, however, the establishment of the Jewish state was only one of the things that had to take place before the Rapture. Those who were astonished by Israel becoming a state grew downright delirious when on June 7, 1967, Israeli troops took East Jerusalem. Fundamentalist and evangelical Christians who believed that this was another incidence of biblical prophecy coming true greeted this victory with triumphant proclamations. Tim LaHaye, Billy Graham, Carl Henry, Pat Robertson, and John Hagee—all preached that the prophecy clock was ticking faster, and the end of history as we know it was at hand. Prophecy conferences in Israel really fired up as evangelical tour groups descended on Tel Aviv in increasing numbers. Renewed interest in Bible prophecy was sparked three years after the capture of East Jerusalem with the first printing of *The Late Great Planet Earth*.

For many premillennialists the seizing of East Jerusalem in 1967 was prophecy coming true, but they hoped for more—the taking of the Temple Mount. The Israeli army, however, held at the Western Wall and didn't take Al-Haram al-Sharif, the Noble Sanctuary, the third-holiest site in Islam, housing the Dome of the Rock, along with the more recent Al Aqsa Mosque. Haram al-Sharif was established in 691 CE, marking the spot where Muhammad ascended to heaven on his nighttime journey from Mecca nearly fourteen hundred years ago. It's also the location where some believe the Second Temple and the Holy of Holies was situated before the destruction of Jerusalem in 70 CE. This contested area holds enormous significance for those who believe the temple needs to be rebuilt. In 1967 there was great anticipation from some Jews and Christians that the moment of divine destiny had come, but they were bitterly disappointed when Israel held the ground it gained and refused to take the Temple Mount.

Why did Israel stop? Was it the smart political decision not to start another holy war? Gershom Gorenberg argues that the reasons for this were not entirely secular, that religious authorities believed that the ritual purification necessary for the third temple to be built was impossible under current conditions. Turns out the world's fate may have depended on the lack of a red heifer. According to Numbers 19, "A red heifer, 'faultless, wherein is no blemish, and upon which came a yoke,' is to be slaughtered and its body burned entirely to ash." Without this purification no one could enter the temple, and the last ashes of a red heifer disappeared with the fall of Jerusalem in 70 CE. Since the biblical text says that anyone who touches death (bone, body, grave) is the same as a dead body and is impure, purification is needed before entering the holy of holies. "The rite of the red heifer, writes Tel

Aviv University's Baruch Schwartz, meant that 'God will dwell among and protect His people' only if death has no dominion in the sanctuary."[7]

Living in the world of Enlightenment rationality and modern science, all this can seem very strange, but red heifers get a lot of attention in certain Christian and Jewish circles. There are people working on cattle breeding specifically for the purposes of creating the red heifer, and back in 1996 excitement arose over Melody, a cow fitting the requirements of the "tenth heifer" who arrives at the time of the Messiah, triggering a moment to rebuild the temple. Some thought this was a fulfillment of prophecy, but one commentator argued that Melody was a "four legged bomb" set to blow up the world if enough people accepted her as a divine sign. Fortunately, Melody turned three and sprouted a few white hairs. For want of a perfect red heifer Armageddon was put on hold.[8]

It's like something out of a Dan Brown novel—dark and shadowy forces, motivated by spiritual agendas, conspire to create a world fit for the return of Christ. We may chuckle at the idea of breeding pure red heifers, but those who are involved in this are absolutely convinced they're serving God. This is why some Jews considered Melody

---

I remember my pastor saying this might be the only reason we should ever scientifically mess with DNA.

THE DEACON

more dangerous than a terrorist. If she had stayed a pure red, expectations would be unleashed in Israel that would have had life-and-death consequences far beyond the precincts of the Temple Mount.

The Hidden Agenda: Turning Jews into Christians

THE ACOLYTE

Exactly how hidden is their agenda?

There are millions of Christians and Jews who believe that Al-Haram al-Sharif is occupied territory that must be destroyed so that the third temple can be rebuilt. The competing claims for this land form a chain linking people and land for thousands of years. Members of each faith community believe their claims are divinely ordained and thus absolute. Unfortunately, compromise seems impossible, leading extremists on all sides to take it upon themselves to do "God's will." Bullet holes in the exterior tiles of the Dome of the Rock, burn marks on the Al Aqsa Mosque, and uncovered plots to blow up the Dome of the Rock are eloquent testimony to the madness of those who would force God's hand in order that prophecy might come true.

This conflict reaches its most intense point when the issue is the temple. The rebuilding of the temple is a deep concern to many in Israel and there are a number of different communities working toward this end. One of the most devout and committed of these groups is the Temple

Institute. A visit to their website offers a window into what motivates those who believe that the restoration of the temple with its priesthood and sacrificial system will bring about the "spiritual well-being of both Israel and all the nations of the world."[9]

This community has scholars who dedicate their efforts to creating the necessary materials and artifacts for the reestablishing of true worship in Israel. Seamless garments of linen woven from a thousand threads, belts of thirty-two cubits, incense shovels, temple vessels, and even red heifers are being worked on so that when the moment comes, they'll be ready to answer the call of God. This type of painstaking detail to ancient patterns, even to the minting of coins that can be used for sacrifice and temple maintenance, reveals something about how our theology shapes us—what we devote our lives to is motivated by who and what we consider God to be.

Even if we admire these efforts, see in them the heart's desire to obey and honor God, there are troubling shadows. In a place where religion, nationalism, and identity swirl in a combustible mix, the belief in biblical prophecy reduces the rationality needed when violence erupts. Casting out all those who do not accept your vision of what God requires leaves you open to the worst type of manipulation—it's them or us. The groups dedicated to rebuilding the temple may exist on the periphery of Israeli society, but given the political situation in Israel, they have the potential to stir a lot of pots.

One of those pots contains the millions of dispensationalists who embrace Christian Zionism. They exist in a world of apocalyptic speculation that interprets Israel through a particular lens, one that has enormous

repercussions for the rest of us. Dispensationalist interpretation mandates that the Temple of Jerusalem be
rebuilt, because this fits their prophetic scenario. This
narrative leads them to form alliances with many in Israel
who see dispensationalists as useful for the accomplish-
ment of their goals. But what gets hidden is *why* dispensationalists welcome the building of the temple. According
to their interpretation, the key verse in this regard is from
the Scofield Bible, where Scofield glosses Daniel 9:27 by
inserting the word "Antichrist" into the text: "And he
(Antichrist) shall confirm the covenant with many for
one week; and in the midst of the week he shall cause the
sacrifice and the oblation to cease, and for the overspread-
ing of abominations he shall make it desolate, even until
the consummation, and that determined shall be poured
upon the desolate."

Darby and Scofield inserted the figure of the Antichrist into Daniel as part of their scheme, which argues
that at the end of days the Antichrist will give Jews the
temple in order that he can desecrate it and wage war on
them. In the middle of the last seven years the Antichrist
kicks things up a notch—especially the body count. In the
dispensational version of the end times Jews are destined
for destruction, stage props for the last act.

Many scholars have noticed that no matter how much
the dispensationalists say they love Jews and Israel; no
matter how many conferences and visits to the Holy Land
they take; the reality is that dispensationalists are continuing a long Christian tradition of anti-Judaism. As we saw
earlier, Darby's interpretation is that God set the Jews
aside when they rejected Christ and launched the Church
Age. This is the dispensation that ends with the Rapture,

followed by the seven-year tribulation, during which time those Jews who accept Jesus as the Messiah will be saved, though they will suffer greatly because of this decision. In other words, at the end of time Jews essentially become . . . Christian. Those Jews who don't accept Jesus as the Messiah in the Great Tribulation once again experience the suffering of not making the "right" choice, and what Lindsey in *The Late Great Planet Earth* calls God's "woodshed" echoes with the screams of the tortured once more. Still, it makes no difference whether Jews decide for or against Jesus as messiah, they're destined to suffer because . . . Revelation. This is a theology that deserves strong critique, because if God is a genocidal maniac, atheism seems the most ethical choice here.

Dispensationalism perpetuates a long and tragic history of Christian supersessionism, where Jews are narrated as actors solely to serve as foils for the Christian story. Jews become important for the dispensationalists as those standing in need of conversion. The eschatological role for the Jews that Christianity has traditionally consigned can only mean death and destruction to those Jews who do not accept Jesus as their messiah. The Jew *qua* Jew vanishes in this form of Christianity, replaced by the Jew who stands as candidate for conversion. The ramifications of this through history have been horrific—pogroms, exile, and the Shoah. If I were Jewish I'd be extremely nervous around those Christians who profess their love for Israel because Jews will help fulfill the prophecies of Christ's return. The dispensational storyline doesn't end well for the Jews, unless you're a Jew for Jesus, in which case everything's cool because you're covered, though you'll still have to suffer.

THE DEACON

A Gentile with a shofar
is always wrong.

What about the Children of Ishmael?

It's not just the Jews who are assigned as props for the end times drama; the children of Ishmael are consigned by dispensationalists to the periphery of God's care and concern. This marginalizing of Arabs has also helped to create the injustices that bedevil Israel today. Millions of Arabs lived in the parts of Palestine that became the State of Israel, and many of them became refugees in 1948. Overnight they lost their land and homes. Two communities of people who have suffered injustice still struggle to find a place for themselves in Israel, and this conflict currently seems incapable of finding any just resolution.

Though seemingly unrelated to Israel's tragedies, the recent Oscar-winning movie *Ida* explores the cost to persons when land and home are taken. At the start of the movie a young woman, Anna, is preparing to take vows to become a nun. She is told by her prioress that she has an aunt, who she must visit. It turns out that Anna's name is actually Ida and her Jewish aunt, Wanda Gruz, has come to share the truth about who Anna/Ida really is. After absorbing the shock of this, Ida and her aunt embark on a road trip to see their former home in Poland, a home that had been taken over by a Polish family that was supposed to hide Ida's family in return for living there, but instead of this mercy they killed Ida's family and put her into the convent. The notion of being an exile, of not having a place to call your own, permeates the movie, and we're not entirely surprised at the tragic consequences of living with this theft of place that colors the narrative. The taking of land and estrangement from the world is known all too well by Jews. It is also known by those living in Palestine in 1948 who had their homes confiscated for no reason other than that someone else mandated it.[10]

Still, the pain of losing home is not entirely lost on those who have benefited from it. Yehezkel and Dalia Landau, religious Zionists whose vision for Zionism includes enfranchised Palestinians, work to create new realities in Israel. In 1967 Dalia discovered that the house she grew up in was the house of an Arab family who had been forcibly evacuated by the Israeli army in 1948. Much like the movie *Ida*, Dalia confronted her past when the Palestinian family came back and asked to visit their home. Eventually Dalia donated the building to found Open House, an organization dedicated to bringing healing and reconciliation between Israeli Jews and Israeli Arabs. There are other such stories of those who are seeking new paths forward motivated by the belief that God wants God's people to live together and flourish.[11]

I think *Ida* is the first movie you've mentioned that I have seen. I promise, dear

THE BISHOP

readers, God raptures no one in the movie.

The hard work of reconciling ourselves to one another in the midst of so much tension is not as exciting as Rayford Steele chasing the Antichrist, Nicolae Carpathia, around the world so that he can assassinate him, but it's no less a reality facing Israel today. Those who fly into Israel, hold prophecy conferences and tours, proclaim their great love for the land, and depart satisfied with their spiritual experience, miss the struggles of people to survive in their daily lives. This hardship is invisible to the casual Christian tourist. The suffering of massive numbers of Palestinians and Jews who do not sit in the seats of power in Israel continues unabated. Apocalyptic scenarios that perpetuate this blindness to suffering are a betrayal of the gospel of Christ.

If purported love of Jews has to be matched by hostility to Muslim or Christian Arabs, then Christianity has learned nothing. Much of this hostility comes from the way that the Bible is read and interpreted in certain Christian communities. The biblical story of Abraham, Sarah, and Hagar is a complicated tale, open to numerous interpretations, not the least of which is how to understand the character of God. But if our identities are shaped by the stories we tell one another, this story doesn't have just one interpretation. God sees and responds to the suffering of Hagar and Ishmael; they're not left alone in exile, and Abraham and Sarah were not blameless. This differs from an interpretation that portrays Hagar as the mother of a community God supposedly doesn't choose. Arab identity is constructed from an ideological reading of the Bible that allows Christians to neglect them as full partners anywhere in the world, just as some Christians read the Bible in a way that neglects Jews as full partners. Connect this to the belief among dispensationalists that the only true faith is Christianity, and the table is set not just for the oppression of Jews, but also for the oppression of Muslims, in particular Arab Muslims.

In dispensational schemes, prophetic beliefs require the elimination of Arabs because they contest giving Israel whatever part of the "Promised Land" they want. Whether it's Hal Lindsey writing about the alliance of the Arab world with communist Russia, or John Hagee weighing in on the hoped-for destruction of all Muslims, the aspirations and lives of millions of people are fit into a scheme of biblical interpretation that does great harm. For example, in a chapter pithily titled "Sheik to Sheik," Lindsey went to great pains forty-five years ago to string biblical passages together to construct a narrative that combines ethnic animosity with a hatred of all things communist to paint a dire picture of the threat Israel faced:

> We have seen how current events are fitting together simultaneously into the precise pattern of predicted events. Israel has returned to Palestine and revived the nation. Jerusalem is under Israeli control. Russia has emerged as a great northern power and is the avowed enemy of revived Israel. The Arabs are joining in a concerted effort to liberate Palestine under Egyptian leadership. The black African nations are beginning to move from sympathy toward the Arabs to an open alliance in their "liberation" cause.[12]

Using texts in Hebrew scripture written in completely different circumstances, dispensationalists cherry pick and then interpret for contemporary readers who have not taken the time to look at any other interpretative grid, a narrative that fits into their ideological world. In this version of the story, everything that has happened or will happen in Israel is due to God's action, which dictates that all who oppose Israel's plans are evil. All Arab presence in Israel, Christian and Muslim, is de facto illegitimate; all other claims to the land are false, even though Arab families have lived there for hundreds of years.

When concerns are raised about the injustice of taking people's homes, the answer is that there never was a Palestinian nation, that the Palestinians are a creation of Arabs who came from other places to live in Israel, and have no rights to the land. In fact, according to the *Left Behind* website, everyone who surrounds Israel is an enemy: "Ezekiel 36–39 clearly calls the people 'the whole House of Israel.' The prophet (inspired by God, who alone can predict history) even provided the names of the enemies of Israel in the end times—the very neighbors of Israel today who continually plot her destruction."[13]

This is not to ignore the fact that Israel truly has enemies who wish it eradicated from the land. This is a reality that must not be hidden in our critique of Christian Zionism. But the religious beliefs of Christians, Muslims, and Jews that God gave the land to a certain group of people for all time doesn't help people on the different sides find any common ground for peaceful coexistence. It's this belief that makes many Muslims, Christians, and Jews so intransigent about potential solutions. The fundamentalists in all three religious communities see the removal of those not of their tribe as the only possible solution. The God of fundamentalism is an idol projected from our fears and anxieties to defeat those we consider enemies.

Despite the compassion
at the heart of every
religion, a fundy can
ruin any of them.

THE ELDER

In fact, most dispensationalist Christians (though not
all) are committed not only to Israeli occupation of Palestinian land, but the erasure of all non-Jews from that land.
This mindset has material effects. John Hagee, one of the
most prominent dispensationalists and a close ally of Shel-
don Adelson, casino owner (because obviously God wants
us to prosper from the broken dreams of desperate people)
and kingmaker of Republican presidential candidates, is
thrilled with the possibility of World War III. After 9/11
he told a BBC radio interviewer, "I believe the world is
going to see an escalation of the Islamic influence all over
the earth, and at that point in time God in his sovereign
grace is going to stand and defend Israel and all the enemies are going to be decimated."[14] God's grace, evidently,
doesn't extend to all, especially those we demonize.

This grace certainly doesn't extend to Palestinian
Christians, people who are marginalized and betrayed
by dispensationalism. These Christians are members of
churches in Israel stretching back to the beginning of
Christianity, but they suffer the occupation of their land.
Their geography is marked by walls and scars in the earth
that unfortunately divide the land between those who
"belong" and those who don't. Roads are monitored, movement is restricted, and freedom is lost for many Christians

who suffer what has happened to Israel. Though some evangelical leaders have recently asked for a more even-handed approach, most dispensationalists believe that all Palestinians—Christian, Muslim, or secular—must either move to Jordan or live under Israeli sovereignty over their land. Because dispensationalists have a particular understanding of what constitutes oppression, Palestinian claims for their rights are seen as illegitimate claims from false brethren.

Many Christians from mainline denominations are increasingly calling for justice for the Palestinians, but these calls are also ignored as coming from the enemy. One of the longstanding aspects of dispensational belief is

THE BISHOP

As a denominational official, of course I am pro-Palestine. But the people I preach to tend to support Zionism.

that anyone who is a part of the mainline denominations is implicitly aligned with Satan, so pleas from Palestinian Christians of Orthodox traditions are obviously bogus. Mainline denominational Christians are regarded with suspicion because they have respect for international law and empathy for the Palestinians. Dispensationalists see any attempt to use government agencies, whether global or national, to resolve conflict and work for peace as a mark of being aligned with the Antichrist. Those who engage in religious efforts like ecumenism or multifaith work also are doing the devil's work, forcing the world into a satanic inspired globalism.[15]

The conservative coalition built around support for Israel is far more powerful than that put together by liberal Christians. It seems that cooperation is only demonic when it comes from liberal or progressive groups. In Jerusalem, for instance, there are a multitude of fundamentalist groups such as the International Christian Embassy, National Religious Broadcasters, and the Christian Family Organization, a group that takes many members of Congress to Israel so that Israel will receive unconditional support from the United States government. Some of these groups have hosted Republican presidential candidates who visit Israel.

But the biggest player in Christian Zionism is the group started by John Hagee, Christians United for Israel, described in some circles as the "Gentile arm" of the American Israel Public Affairs Committee (AIPAC). Benjamin Netanyahu said of them, "I consider CUFI to be a vital part of Israel's national security." This group has been at the forefront of efforts to make sure that the right wing of Israel has the ability to do whatever it desires, and in that they have been very effective.

The Enemy of My Enemy Is My Friend . . . Or Not

The totality of dispensational commitment to Israel means that no other legitimate moral claims exist outside of whatever it is that Israel deems necessary. For many dispensationalists the God-given boundaries of Israel stretch from the Nile to the Euphrates. The most strident believe all this land will be annexed and all Palestinians will be driven from their homes. This means that the continuing occupation of Palestinian land and homes is ignored by the 82 percent of white evangelicals who believe God gave the land to Israel. This is the point where end times theology becomes destructive—dispensationalists will justify anything Israel's government does, no matter what it is.

Not a few Israeli leaders see in these expressions of unqualified support a powerful tool to leverage American opinion, and this support factors into Israel's political calculations. From the beginning in 1948, Israeli leaders cultivated relationships between evangelical Christians and Israel, even as its leaders were mystified by the biblical interpretations of their new friends. In 1971 David Ben-Gurion welcomed the Jerusalem prophecy conference, giving official recognition to the dispensationalists. Likewise, Israel's U.S. ambassador, Chaim Herzog, gave an interview for the film version of *The Late Great Planet Earth*. Subsequent prophecy tours by Hagee, Lindsey, and numerous others have received a warm welcome by the highest-ranking Israeli officials.[16] The only exception to this is when someone other than the hard right wing is in office.

While American evangelicals extended unqualified love to Israel, that love can wax and wane, depending on the political leanings of Israel's leadership. Israel's more expansionist leaders are cheered by dispensationalists with every incursion into what is considered the boundaries of God's promise. In 1982 when Israel invaded Lebanon in order to create a safe zone in the north of Israel and clear out the PLO from that area, evangelical Christians sprung into action, taking out ads in the *New York Times*, holding rallies at the White House, and launching letter-writing campaigns by those who believed that the invasion was in fulfillment of biblical prophecy. There were, however, few if any evangelical voices that mourned the high number of civilian causalities or the massacre at the Sabra and Shatila camps in West Beirut.

It's what Israel calls "disputed" land, the West Bank and East Jerusalem, where current conflicts are most intense. Israeli settlers have built communities on Palestinian land occupied by Israel in the 1967 war. Considered illegal under international law, these settlements are being built to create a situation "on the ground" that will make a Palestinian state impossible. This disenfranchisement of Palestinians is desired by dispensationalists, even to the point of linking evangelical congregations with sister Israeli settlements. The Israeli settlements are not interpreted as squatters encroaching on land that doesn't belong to them, but as the necessary fulfillment of biblical prophecy. When Israel's government supports these moves, dispensationalists cheer them on.

If, however, an Israeli government takes power that is considered too liberal, dispensationalists reveal their dark side. When Yitzhak Rabin's government dealt with Palestinian issues through working on the Oslo Accord, it did so on the basis of an honest appraisal of security concerns, which meant they were open to the idea of exchanging land for lasting peace. Many dispensational evangelicals cooled to any concessions offered in order to make peace. In his 1996 best-seller, *Beginning of the End: The Assassination of Yitzhak Rabin and the Coming Antichrist*, John Hagee argued that Israel was divided between secular and religious Jews, with only one group having faith in the God of the Jews. Putting Rabin's assassination into this context, he claimed that Yigal Amir, Rabin's assassin, belonged to the religious side of Israel (spoiler alert: the good side). Hagee was joined by others like Pat Robertson, who speculated that Rabin's assassination and Ariel Sharon's stroke happened because both men pursued policies of "dividing God's land."[17] Evidently God, like the mafia, sometimes has to "send a message."

The connection between dispensationalism and right-wing politics has been tight since the inception of the doctrine, and its manifestations in Israeli and American politics have had significant consequences in our time. Nowhere is this more apparent than the life and career of Benjamin Netanyahu, who has courted evangelical leaders throughout his career. He has also encouraged the efforts of those in Israel who want Haram al-Sharif to revert to Jewish hands.[18]

Christians who profess such love for Jews are questionable allies. As stated earlier, dispensationalists' excitement over the third temple is not due to the restoration of ancient Jewish religious identity; they're excited because it signals the beginning of the end. The restoration of the temple is an occasion for the death of two-thirds of Israel according to the dispensationalists. Among those like Lindsey, Hagee, and others of their ilk, this is not in doubt. They believe there is hope in Jews suffering chastisement, because this motivates them to turn to God. Dispensationalist theology envisions a God who is severe and punishing, using any number of biblical passages to address Israel's coming judgment: "And just as the LORD took delight in making you prosperous and numerous, so the LORD will take delight in bringing you to ruin and

Isn't a bit problematic
that the Zionists are nicer
to Israel than their God
is going to be?

THE ACOLYTE

destruction; you shall be plucked off the land that you are
entering to possess" (Deuteronomy 28:63). Like the ultimate domestic abuser; God only beats you for your own
good. God destroys because God loves. As horrific as this
sounds, it's a guiding biblical principle for millions.

The horrific loss of life at the end of days comes with a
Catch-22 that's almost impossible to overcome. Jews make
an alliance with the Antichrist to rebuild the temple, but
after forty-two months the Antichrist puts his image in
the temple, demanding worship. This opens the eyes of a
remnant of Jews to reject the Antichrist in favor of the
true messiah: "The tribulation will definitely be a part
of Israel's sorrowful and tragic history. . . . The unbelief
and failures of Israel are pruned and punished through
the unparalleled fires of tribulation. The Jewish remnant
entering the millennium at the end of the tribulation will
thus have been purified for the kingdom."[19]

So, to recap—the fate of Jews in the end times script
means that they suffer at Satan's hands, because Satan hates
the chosen, but it's God's loving justice that destroys over
two-thirds of the Jews. Jews are going to suffer because
they worship the Antichrist; Jews are going to suffer for
refusing to bow down to the beast. The bottom line is that
Jews are going to suffer eternal damnation because they
didn't make the "right" choice by accepting Jesus as their

Messiah, or they're also going to suffer horribly when they finally do make the "right" choice after the Rapture. Jews have been suffering at Christian hands for not making the "right" choice ever since the Jewish and Christian communities ended up disconnected from one another. Talk about a "lose-lose" scenario.

In this theology, Jews are situated in such a way that they are foils for the ultimate triumph of Christianity. Despite professing such great love for Israel, dispensationalists embrace a story that leads to the destruction of Jews. Nowhere in dispensational literature does this interpretation allow for the fact that religious Jews have the integrity of their own faith, should be respected, and not viewed with condescension and paternal regret at their impending doom: "A theology that says that Jews as a community have denied God in the past and are destined to be punished in the future is hardly free of anti-Semitism."[20]

Israel and all those who live there are part of a drama, but that drama plays out in a far different register than dispensationalist Christians believe. Jews, Christians, and Muslims all exist on the same piece of land and perhaps The End is not what we envision. As we contemplate the power of endings, we should give thought to beginnings as well. Unspooling this tangled web of relationships, we're confronted with stories that narrate a God who grants land, which for those who are promised it, is great. But we should consider the claims of those who already lived there. In wondering how we got to where we are, and where we are going, we must now look at where we started. We turn our gaze to ancient Israel.

Back to the Future

Some of these things were fulfilled at that time, while some others were fulfilled later on, and others are left for the time of the King-Messiah. . . . We have learned that the Holy One, Blessed Be He, will rebuild Jerusalem and will reveal one fixed star that shoots seventy mobile stars, and seventy sparks that are illumined from this star [are found] at the center of the firmament. . . . In that time the star will expand and become visible over the world and then mighty wars will arise in all the four quarters of the world and faith is going to be absent among them.

Zohar, vol. 3, fol. 212b

T he week I started work on this chapter, the Church of the Multiplication of Loaves and Fishes, one of the most famous Catholic Churches in the Holy Land, was set ablaze in the middle of the night. The church, located on the shores of Galilee in northern Israel, marks the traditional spot where Jesus multiplied the loaves and fishes.

Graffiti with the words, "And false idols will be smashed" was found scrawled in red spray paint on a wall outside of the church. Initial suspicion pointed to extremist Israeli settlers who are implicated in a number of attacks recently on both Muslim mosques and Christian churches. According to *Haaretz*, since 2011 there have been seventeen such attacks on Muslim and Christian holy spaces. Though Israeli officials were quick to condemn the attack, the Catholic Church in Israel complained that the government had not dealt adequately with the last four years of attacks by extremist settlers. Many Jews are horrified by these acts, but they continue even as Chief Sephardic Rabbi Yitzhak Yosef criticized them: "The deviant behavior of church arsonists in the north must be condemned absolutely, and they should be punished severely."[1]

These attacks are happening at the same time that tensions continue to rise on the Temple Mount where emotions are flaring between Arabs and Jews who are caught in the cycle of violence and retribution that eats away at Israeli and Palestinian society. Given the intractable nature of the situation, the issue of whether the status quo on the Temple Mount can be maintained, or whether Jerusalem will soon erupt into another hot zone of religious and sectarian conflict, becomes increasingly urgent. Those committed to a dispensational perspective welcome any event that will disrupt the status quo because no matter how horrific for the citizens of Israel and Jerusalem, destruction of what presently stands on the Temple Mount fits their end times scenario for the building of the third temple.

Secularists often look at these events and scratch their heads, wondering why people get so worked up about religion, but those involved in this dispute believe something vital to their very lives is at stake—this continual tension goes to the heart of personal and corporate identity. Stop for a moment and think about how you feel when your faith or beliefs are questioned. Some people get defensive. But it's when we really question things, take a close look at how we came to believe certain ideas as true and others as false, that our life changes. It's important to know about beginnings when we're contemplating The End.

Back to the Start

As counterintuitive as this sounds, to understand a small bit about Israel's beginnings can offer us some wisdom about how we think of endings. One reason for this, as we've already seen, is that Jewish writers shaped our apocalyptic imagination. Christianity cannot understand itself without grasping its Jewish roots. In order to gain a bit of perspective, we're going to have to consider how religion shapes cultural identity (if you're particularly narcissistic just substitute "me" for cultural identity going forward and it will still make sense, I hope), because while there are many secular Jews, Israel itself can only be understood by the call of God, a religious idea. I'm going to be asking you to do some serious thinking for the next few minutes and you may find yourself disagreeing strongly. That's a good thing, because what I'm going to lay out is likely to be hotly contested depending on how you understand faith. So, take your time, grab some sustenance, maybe a cool and refreshing adult beverage to wash down your cheesy poofs, snacky cakes, and chocolate-covered chicken potpies and let's get started.

THE DEACON

No Hummus?!
I thought progressive
Christians had to snack
on hummus?!

People often grow nervous when they first confront the fact that religion is a human construction, built over thousands of years of ritual, myth, and culture. This flies in the face of the reality that many people of faith consider their origins rooted in the experience of individuals and communities with God. For those who are more fundamentalist in orientation, all other contextual concerns such as history and social location are not considered important for understanding faith. Some people even think that consideration of contextual factors when we explore religion is a threat to faith. Religion, though, is a multifaceted phenomenon with many dimensions, all of which serve to give us a richer picture. The realization that we create what goes by the title of *religion* gives us even more interesting things to consider.

As indicated previously, our religious stories shape our identity and create in us a sense of what home looks like. For example, across the globe, origin stories locate us in the universe, tell us who we are, and what our purpose is. Where did we come from? We came from God, who created us in God's image; or perhaps we came from the mud of the ocean, the sand under the Great Turtle's nails. Those who embrace these stories often internalize them to such an extent that they are no longer just stories, but the truth about life. We become committed to these stories, often to the exclusion of those who have different stories. This is not just the case with the Jewish story, but the Christian story, the Muslim story, and all the other stories we share. It is stories and narratives that help us shape our reality.

With so many neighbors of different faiths I have always wondered who really believes their story

THE ACOLYTE

is THE story. Not who says it, but believes when no one is looking.

Since religion takes our contingent and transitory life and roots it in transcendent reality, religious stories acquire a unique authority. Because of ancient stories, Israel is seen not just as a piece of land on the Mediterranean; Israel, and especially Jerusalem, is the center of the world. This is an idea that has shaped Jewish consciousness since the stories of Abraham and Moses were first written down. Jewish existence would be unthinkable outside the call of Abraham, the covenant of Moses, or Saul, David, Solomon, and the monarchy. The religious shaping of human life raises questions about how societies develop over time, and how certain aspects of that development, for example monotheism, emerge to shape cultures (me). To the person of faith, such developments happen because humans encounter the God who reveals Godself, and these revelations become narrated through time. Whether it's a burning bush, or a still small voice, religious stories serve as vehicles of revelation about the Creator.

However, we tend to view the unfolding of human history, one thing is certain—societies are formed over time for purposes of survival and protection. What is striking about this is that as we read the earliest stories known to us, the element of religion, specifically the connection between human creations and divine origin, was present from the very beginning. Religion legitimated and justified whatever human structures emerged over time. Sometimes these orders were closely identified with natural forces, but at some point religion became employed to justify political structures. If chaos was an ever-present threat, fusion between god and king established order, just as the proper performance of ritual kept balance. God had established an order, or gave a king to lead, and it was up to the people to follow God's law. All ancient and archaic cultures, Israel included, had their own way of making these connections.

Right about now you may be asking yourself, "Is this guy saying there's nothing to religion other than what we create?" This guy's not saying that, but he is asking you to consider that much of what we think of as "revelation" can be muddled with our own ideas about what God should be like and whom God should love or even hate. All of us participate in this process of reading God's story into our lives.

THE BISHOP

This is why religious leaders need to be aware and responsible to our role in the process.

Who Is Telling This Story?

When we read the biblical account of Israel's formation we find a dramatic narrative, put together over hundreds of years by many different authors who changed the story, embellished it, created new stories, or rewrote new versions of old stories to make a certain claim about what Israel was. Basically, the outlines are that God called Abraham to be the father of a great nation in a land that God would give to Abraham and his descendants, containing so many people they would be like the grains of sand on a beach (Genesis 12:1–3). Due to famine, however, Abraham's children had to migrate to Egypt, where they suffered in slavery until God called Moses to deliver the children of Israel from the oppression of Pharaoh. After forty years in the wilderness, they entered into their Promised Land and conquered the tribes who would not worship the one true God. Eventually they established a monarchy, built a temple for God, and constantly fought off threats to their existence. Over times of crisis, such as the exile into Babylon in 587/6 bce, or the sack of Jerusalem in 70 ce and the diaspora of Jews throughout the world, Jews have kept faith with God, though the form of that faith has changed significantly over time.

The story of Israel is a narrative that shapes the world to the extent that it's impossible to understand the history of Western civilization without Israel. Judaism, Christianity, and Islam would not exist without this story. Yet, according to the archaeological record, the narrative I just gave is not entirely an accurate story. Archaeology and other investigations tell a more complex story of diverse peoples in Palestine who become joined together by a covenant that has the form of other nations' covenants. These other covenants were agreements about responsibilities that existed between rulers and subjects. Israel's covenant, however, differed in that God was the ruler and Israel, God's subject.

Israel emerged from a multitude of tribes in the hill country of northern Palestine. While difficult to give a complete account of this, we can tease out from Judges and 1 Samuel that the early societies were organized around kinship, clans, and tribes, with no real stable structure above the tribal level. In this milieu many gods existed and were worshiped, many of them having to do with fertility and nature. The original god of Israel was Elohim, the El above all other Els, a generic West Semitic term for god, spirit, or ancestor.[2] The tribal communities that would become Israel were enmeshed within a world of many Els and even Yahwehs. In most of those communities the earthly ruler was designated so by the God his tribe served.

It was this fact, that Israel was surrounded by cultures who had already solidified the connection between kings and the gods who fought for them, which led to the eventual adoption of Yahweh as the patron of Israel's fledgling monarchy. Walter Brueggemann calls our attention to the way in which Israel's move to a monarchy changed the consciousness of people and led to different convictions about how society should be constructed. One of these paths protected the status of the monarchy and its inherent nationalism; the other, more prophetic in outlook, continually called the monarchy and all that went with it into question. Brueggemann uses the dichotomy of "royal" and "prophetic" consciousness to probe the different ideologies that shaped Israel during the writing of the Pentateuch and other Hebrew scripture, but we should be wary of hard-and-fast binaries in this dividing of consciousness.[3] While these two streams of thought are pres-

---

I hope anyone involved in a church takes this tension into their leadership.

THE BISHOP

---

ent in the various narratives of Hebrew scripture, they often intersect and play off of one another depending on who is telling the story. Sometimes the prophets can be very supportive of the temple, though the monarchy's attempt to use the temple to legitimate power is always a bit suspect.

One of the most profound implications of this tension is that those writers of the biblical texts who supported the rise of the monarchy through Saul, David, Solomon, and beyond, embraced the idea that God legitimated the establishment of the monarchy and all that went with it. So, for example, God establishes the king, and the king repays the favor by building God a house. It's not hard to see how this shapes feelings about the land. If the land was taken from others and given to the children of Abraham by God, then that land becomes inviolate. God set God's people there, and God, like the deities of other nations, would fight for God's people: "But if the king of Judah was the Lord's anointed and Yahweh ruled over all the gods, then, in principle, all the nations must bow down to Zion."[4]

This creates a certain consciousness about what Israel is, what Jerusalem is, and what their meaning will be for subsequent generations. No matter how things are conceived politically in the present day, this ancient history drives the actions of millions. If you've made it this far you may be feeling pretty resistant to where this is going. Worse, you may think this replicates the serpent's question in the Garden of Eden: "Did God truly say . . . ?" In the interest of full disclosure, I am, in fact, arguing that the narrative of Israel that drives dispensationalists can also be read as a story certain human beings created to justify royal politics and that a closer look at how faith was being defined in ancient Israel might offer different paths of interpretation.

David's bringing the ark of God to Jerusalem and claiming Yahweh as the God of his kingship, as well as Solomon's building of the temple, were interpreted by some biblical writers as in accordance with divine will. The order of the world connected God and Israel's monarchy in this theology. However, it may not be as simple as God ordaining the temple, especially when some scholars have shown how deeply indebted Solomon was to pagan ideas when he built his temple:

> Solomon's temple was built on the regional model and its furniture showed how thoroughly the cult of Yahweh had accommodated itself to the pagan landscape of the Near East. There was clearly no sectarian intolerance in Israelite Jerusalem. At the temple's entrance were two Canaanite standing stones (*matzevoth*) and a massive bronze basin, representing Yam, the sea monster fought by Baal, supported by twelve

brazen oxen, common symbols of divinity and fertility. The temple rituals too seem to have been influenced by Baal's cult in neighboring Ugarit.[5]

In other words, this temple was built during a time when Solomon pursued aims that mirrored other cultures that also constructed their social orders on an immanent, constituent connection between heaven and earth, represented in king and temple. These other cultures also built into their system a structural and systemic violence that used people as slaves to serve the rulers.

Luckily America was built by Christian missionaries in very loving ways. #CityOnAHill #sarcasm

THE ELDER

Solomon was not immune from the same temptation. 1 Kings gives ample evidence that the securing of Solomon's leadership was accomplished by the development of an elaborate bureaucracy to institutionalize technical reason, the forming of a standing army, removing military action from the community's consent; conscripted labor to build the inevitable manifestations of empire, and the development of tax districts to help pay for the royal cities, palaces, and the temple. All of this supposedly supported and legitimated by God.[6] If there had been a Hebrew Tea Party back in the day, they would've opposed all of this, unless, of course, they ran things; then they might enjoy having that army.

The complexity of this supposed connection between God and Israel, however, is seen in the biblical counter-narrative. One of the most profound critiques of Israel's move to a monarchy was recorded in 1 Samuel 8 when Samuel warned Israel that kings would build armies and drain resources away from the people to wage war, enslaving men and women alike to satisfy their desire for conquest and opulent living (the more things change, the more they stay the same, huh?). The choosing of a king by Israel was seen by the author of 1 Samuel 8:6–18 as a mark of unfaithfulness, not glory. In other words, what we read in the Bible sometimes is not as simple as we think it is. Just because someone does something and says God is involved doesn't necessarily make it so, and plenty of writers critiqued what their leaders were up to.

Hebrew scripture gives ample evidence that the monarchy brought all the social ills that Samuel warned about. The energies and lives of people were put in service to building an empire, one manifestation of which was Solomon's temple. Social oppression became one of the daily marks of existence as the strength of the state became the absolute and total goal of life. Simply put, not everyone in Israel accepted the monarchy as the will of God. This is seen by the fact that another tradition, the prophetic, arose to contest the monarchy.

Samuel's warning anticipated ongoing tensions among the people of Israel. The building of the temple, meant as an expression of primacy and might, signified Yahweh's approval of Solomon's rule. Another interpretation may have seen this as something more tragic—the loss of God's freedom. Numerous conflicts exist throughout the Bible as humankind worked out its theology, one of these being the space between God's accessibility and God's freedom. The building of a temple, connecting royal rule with priests and rituals, spoke for the desires of the monarchy, but it also constituted a religious world little different from Israel's surrounding neighbors.

The moment God becomes the possession of a political order and the religious ideology that supports it, we're no longer talking about God, but the end of our own desires. The biblical texts arguing for the monarchy are

---

Now that makes sense. I just wonder if the water between the divine and our desires is always too muddy.

THE ACOLYTE

---

evidence that a type of religious consciousness depends on the assumption that what exists is the way God wishes it to be. No deep questioning about the orders that shape society are allowed. This is the way that social order imposes itself on us most powerfully: the idea that what we're enmeshed in is true reality and any questioning of it is foolish, dangerous even, because questions are an offense against the Almighty.

There are outcomes to having God rubber stamp our desires. One of these, previously mentioned, was the notion that Jerusalem itself was inviolate and only meant for one people, the ones who owned it. If the Lord of Hosts rules to the end of the earth (Psalm 46:10), then the hegemony of this Lord is limitless. Everything belongs to this Lord. "In the Near Eastern royal tradition, the great king, the king of kings, is, in principle the ruler of the cosmos."[7] This is a universal claim with consequences not just for Israel, but the entire world. The question of who owns what represents the very definition of what faith looks like. We're currently confronted with two very different, but no less absolute claims represented by Muslims about al Haram al-Sharif and Jews about the Temple Mount. These are ultimately religious assertions and, as such, resist reconciliation. I'm arguing that we should see these claims as relative to the communities that first created the stories that justified taking land, and yes, I realize that for some this is an outlandish challenge. But if we're thinking about how to negotiate claims to the land, how we did it in the past counts, right?

If you truly believe, as the dispensationalists do, that God gave Israel a certain spot of land, then that promise is still in effect because royal theology serves a timeless God, whose will never changes. Israel is not only a manifestation of the will of past political and state actors; it's the continuing will of God to conquer all enemies, no matter the costs to others. Such claims are rooted in divine fiat that extend from the beginning of time to the end of days; they transcend history and perhaps for that very reason should be regarded with suspicion. Once political power attaches itself to divine legitimation, no other claim can demand a hearing. *Deus dixit*, God has spoken. Like the bumper sticker seen on more cars than we should hope for: "God said it. I believe it. That settles it."

The idea that you and your community are entitled to someone else's land because God said so has been one of the most powerful excuses throughout history for stealing what others have. This religious legitimation is not found just in Judaism, it's a guiding force in Christianity from the time of Constantine and in Islam from the time of its founding. All monotheistic religions can be critiqued as providing legitimation for taking what others had, especially in the belief that "God" gave it to them, or that the "pagans" needed the blessings of the true God. The Crusades, Conquistadores, the Americas—all of these histories are tied to colonial and imperial pretensions in the name of God.

This certainty reflects an attitude that willingly accepts the connection between political power and divine existence. What some of the prophets of Israel argued, however, was that the acceptance of an order where the king mediates God's presence blinds us to the untold and hidden cost to lives who sacrifice daily so that the order can be maintained. Religion becomes the very thing that prevents us from seeing the enormous price people pay when the dominant powers demand resources and lives be spent in maintaining the order that exists. The beliefs of dispensationalists are totalizing to the extent that oppressive social orders are justified by the type of religious legitimation that was judged and found wanting by many of Israel's own prophets.

What Manner of Person Is the Prophet?

Though with a history as complicated as that of Israel and Judah I hesitate to make overly sweeping statements, I think it's fair to argue that the critique of a society that oppresses the stranger or the sojourner came from within Israel's people, not their rulers. The questioning of the human costs of the monarchy is a strong tradition in the Bible, but it's this very imperial consciousness that currently motivates Christian Zionism. Accepting an incomplete understanding of what Israel is, and what God's justice might look like, they justify the horrible treatment of millions of Palestinians and perpetuate the continuing injustice of a Christianity that believes it should be a triumphant force in the world. In the world of end times doctrines, this is without a doubt the dominant voice in America's political landscape.

As we think about eschatology and apocalypse, especially as it relates to dispensational theology and its embrace of Christian Zionism, we have resources in the prophetic traditions for responding to current struggles. There is no unified voice in scripture that offers God's definitive justification for conquest. A counternarrative is always present. In both Jewish and Christian scriptures, God had many interpreters. How we discern the truth and authenticity of God in this cacophony of voices has been faith's continual pilgrimage.

Finished those cheesy poofs yet? Maybe it's time for some snacky cakes before we continue. For those reading on Kindle, hopefully none of this has angered you enough to throw the thing at the wall.

The journey of faith unfolds in distinct landscapes. For Israel, the terrain has been littered with war, hostility, and recurring destruction, an experience Jews do not wish to repeat. In 587/6 BCE and 70 CE the worst blow to Israel was seeing the sanctity of Jerusalem wounded by the destruction of the great symbol of Israel's power, the temple. Though there was an appreciation for what the temple stood for among the prophets, the voices of critique were raised when the rulers didn't pursue the moral vision the prophets proclaimed, and the temple stood for nothing other than Israel's power.

The prophets created an alternative consciousness to the monarchies that dominated Israel and Judah. They evoked a different reality and relationship between God and people as they responded to the suffering unleashed by the tremendous pressures of Assyrian and Babylonian military and political power. It was this suffering that gave rise to the prophetic imagination, to critiques of kings and the oppression they bring. A call to worship Yahweh alone, an implicit rejection of all syncretism between royal gods and subject peoples, is a call to drop the self-deception behind all theologies that justify the oppression of others. The prophets ask us to imagine what a new relationship with God might look like.

One example of this can be seen in Jeremiah, living near the Babylonian exile and fall of Jerusalem in 587/6 BCE. His grief is overwhelming as he mourns the loss of his world, but he's never without a question for that world as well: "Is there no balm in Gilead? Is there no physician here?" (Jeremiah 8:22). The structures that previously existed, that might have responded to the brokenness Jeremiah mourns, have dissipated. The end is upon him and his people. The remarkable thing is that even in the midst of what felt like the end of his world, Jeremiah confronts those who trust in the temple or believe they can find the Lord there:

> The word that came to Jeremiah from the Lord: Stand in the gate of the Lord's house, and pro-claim there this word, and say, Hear the word of the Lord, all you people of Judah, you that enter these gates to worship the Lord. Thus says the

> Lord of hosts, the God of Israel: Amend your ways
> and your doings, and let me dwell with you in this
> place. Do not trust in these deceptive words: "This
> is the temple of the Lord, the temple of the Lord,
> the temple of the Lord." (Jeremiah 7:1–4)

What follows is a call to act justly, not oppress the widow, the orphan, or the alien, and to put away the worship of other gods who were really no gods. Later, following a biblical pattern of God's judgment and then reconciliation, Jeremiah proclaims the restoration of Israel, but this is a future rooted in people who follow righteousness (Jeremiah 33:14–16). If a new temple emerges, it will be one that doesn't serve the needs of kings.

A theme running through Israel's prophets is the hope for a future where all things, not just human beings, are transformed into a new creation. This was the eschatological horizon that stood at the end of their world. For millions today who anticipate Christ's return, what stands at the end of our world looks far different: death, destruction, falling planes, crashing cars, and the triumphant reign of a tribal god who cleanses instead of redeems. Thug Jesus, meet gangsta God. Recovery of a prophetic critique offers us much as we negotiate religion's intractable demands. If

---

THE DEACON

Oddly enough it was a week after I recovered the prophetic critique that I lost my youth ministry job.

the relationship between God and humankind is understood as a continuing struggle of faith to live in obedience to God, we should put away the simplistic ideas of Christ's return that dominate contemporary culture in America.

When we do, we might find a different perspective to consider. For example, what are we to do with the prophet's warning about the demands that royal consciousness places on people? Jeremiah proclaimed that God desired a reconfigured humanity, a creature whose heart would be changed by the willingness to leave behind the false security of the king to embrace the covenant that should have defined Israel. This fresh rendering of the covenant reorders existence: "But this is the covenant that I will make with the house of Israel after those days, says the LORD: I will put my law within them, and I will write it on their hearts; and I will be their God, and they shall be my people" (Jeremiah 31:33).

This vision saw the relationship with God rooted in the human experience that, while fragile, is more resilient than the contingencies of history. If Ezekiel believed the day was coming when the enemies of Israel would be destroyed (38–39) and the temple rebuilt (40–48), he also proclaimed that God desires we have a different kind of heart: "A new heart I will give you, and a new spirit I will put within you; and I will remove from your body the heart of stone and give you a heart of flesh" (Ezekiel 36:26).

Taking the Road Less Traveled

This drives us to the mystery of what being *chosen* means. Israel's identity as being chosen shouldn't mean the exclusion of all those who are not Jews from the land, just as

Christianity shouldn't legitimate the oppression of others in the name of "civilization." A new heart doesn't desire the destruction of so many neighbors so you can take their land, or if it does, then I confess I'm an atheist to the God who demands such things. Though there are some biblical passages that might indicate this very thing, the desire to dominate is countered throughout scripture with another vision, the call of the prophets for a new heart, and a deeper understanding of where covenant with God takes us. The prophets criticized those who practiced sacrifice and worship of God that was not accompanied by this deeper moral understanding of the covenant. My argument is that religion doesn't have to propel us on a trajectory of hatred, exclusion, and taking over territory from others because your theology legitimates it. That's the royal consciousness at work.

THE ACOLYTE

If the version of religion that doesn't suck is always the "road less traveled," why not just drop religion altogether?

From the earliest days when Israel was but a loose collection of tribal peoples in Palestinian hill country, alternative ways of response were put before the community. One path leads to kings (or politicians) who rule over you, of needing to love the king (president or prime minister) in order that you might not have to eat lentils all your life (though lentils can be quite good, especially with butter, or a bit of kale and hot sauce). This path results in giving allegiance to the questionable goals and immoral ends of the monarchy. This has a clear trajectory not only through Israel's history, but within Christianity, which has also embraced the false idols of political power and dominance, even to the point of baptizing the death of millions throughout history with the justification of God's will.

Those most familiar with the background, history, and production of scriptures know that this destructive track is found in the Bible. From the warnings against monarchy, to the fall of Israel into monarchy, radical voices, branded as treasonous by their rulers, were able to break free from this imposed reality to question whether the way Israel had taken was God's will. Some of Israel's prophets offered an alternative vision. This vision was not the one where God functioned as the legitimation of social order, but upended social order in favor of a renewed heart that would demand a deeper justice for the vulnerable and dispossessed.

In imperial theology the king (or whoever rules) stands at the center and all institutions serve to legitimate the ruler, because that person keeps you safe. The religious order cultivates priests (and prophets) who tell a fearful and terrified population that God ordained all the oppression that is happening to them. The economic order constitutes itself so that all serve the needs of the master, thus ensuring slavery of some sort will be ongoing. And, yes, even here, eschatological claims are made. Davidic royal theology made a claim about the Messiah that has shaped Jewish and Christian apocalypses, and informs contemporary Christian thinking about who Jesus is and what is to be expected at his return.

THE DEACON

This reminds me of the Alfred North Whitehead quote about Caesar's editors getting ahold of Christianity and reworking for Empire.

What gives us pause here is the connection between apocalypse and violence in this theology. At the end the Lamb brings violence and destruction. These images have become so much a part of us that we cannot even conceptualize The End without horrific violence, a cleansing, purifying violence that destroys our enemies and puts all that is wrong with the world right. Whether you read Revelation as political prophecy or a forecast of the future, at the very least you should pay attention to the fact that it's the Lamb, not humankind, who employs violence. Christians have a decision to accept or reject the political death cults that seek to grab from the Lamb the justification for their oppressive violence.

Another scenario, represented in Israel's history by prophetic critique, narrates a different reality—an alternative community of justice and mercy. In the struggle to define the relationship between God and humankind, the prophets challenged a social order built on the systemic violence of political rule. Kings and presidents have no monopoly on God. No temple can contain the wild freedom of God to love what or whom God has chosen. Of course, those who have suffered at the hands of others, especially Christian others, are perfectly justified in inter-rogating me:

"Who are you, sitting in your comfortable home with food and drink, to tell us what the prophets mean and how we should live?"

"I'm not trying to tell you how to live. I'm only sug-gesting that the way we've ordered the world leads to nothing but continuing pain for everyone."

"Easy for you to say, but I challenge you again: What gives you the right to question how we secure our space in the world? Did you lose your grandparents in the fur-nace? Was your life destroyed for simply being a Jew? Are you surrounded by enemies that wish nothing other than your destruction? Enough with your liberal fantasies!"

Rubbing hands on leg. "I don't mean to minimize your suffering, only to suggest that the prophets offered us a way that gives us possibilities beyond endless conflict and death."

"You have no right to our prophets, or to judge us. At least the dispensationalists are helping us in our struggles."

"I understand you think so, but they're shaky allies who have other types of agendas for your erasure."

"Perhaps so, but as long as they fight with us against our enemies we'll stick with them and not you and your tedious concerns with the prophetic."

Suffering is the truth behind this challenge, and Christians must respond to these questions with confes-sion for the ways that they have added to the suffering of others. Christianity after Auschwitz still has much to answer for in this regard. It's important that we resist all those who would seek to harm Jews, but prophetic resis-tance addresses the oppression of all those—Palestinian,

Muslim, Jew, Christian, and atheist—who were created in the image of God. Love is a universal claim.

Those who would destroy the sacred spaces of others have been captured by Revelation's beast. Those who believe that the erasure and destruction of enemies is the only way to survive will continue to wander in the wilderness. Try as we might to reject this, we often live out of the logic of the beast and not of God, especially in our passionate embrace of an apocalypse that will destroy our enemies and restore us as rulers of the earth.

When the prophets of the north and south called Israel and Judah to another vision of life, they did so suffering in the midst of exile and surrounded by those kingdoms that continually threatened their people. Assyria, Babylon, Greece, Rome—all the beasts found in Jewish apocalypses—dominated Israel. Even within the belly of these beasts some of the prophets believed that God was stronger than political orders and that true strength came from obedience to a deeper life than political expediency. This prophetic response seems like weakness, but it can be the most divine—and subversive—way to defeat enemies. The best way to resist empires is not to become like them; the oppression of others eats at your soul, turning you into the very thing you hate. This was the warning of the prophets. It's a word that gets lost today because it's perceived as weak and worthless in the world we live in.

If Israel's prophets envisioned a dismantling of all those orders that enslaved people in the name of divine command, then perhaps that is the task of our age—the imagining of new realities in constructing the world. In the midst of apocalyptic rhetoric and the choosing of sides in anticipation of the last battle, the prophets continue to confront us with where we're taking the world. We should fight for a world where the sacred spaces of others are not burnt to the ground, where faith is not the absolute possession of one people, and destruction of the planet is not a preordained fate. Prophetic consciousness envisions a world where we'll have the courage to donate our home in order to reconcile with our enemies. Yehezkel and Dalia Landau point us to the truth that we can either bulldoze to rubble the homes of our enemies, or we can work to secure space for reconciliation and peaceful lives. One of these paths leads to continual prison, the other to freedom; one of these roads takes us to Armageddon, the other to New Jerusalem.

The End Is a Destination Not Yet Fixed

Earth is careening toward its final act—are you prepared?

John Hagee, *Earth's Final Moments*, 2011

The images both horrified and intrigued us: bodies lying scattered like discarded dolls on the jungle floors of Jonestown, Guyana; roaring flames engulfing the Branch Davidian compound in Waco, Texas; Converse sneakers on the eerie, still bodies hoping to enter Heaven's Gate lying on bunks in San Diego. These are not the only images we struggle to make sense of. We fail to understand the suicide bomber expecting a better life after the fire and ashes settle on the floor, or the assassins of Jewish leaders shouting the name of God before they put another bullet into the world. These succumbed to the siren call of The End. In the face of so much destruction we scratch our heads, perplexed by those who believe that the sweet by-and-by necessitates the destruction of the bitter here and now. The End is terrifying. Or, at least, that is what some would have us think.

The way apocalyptic expectation has been framed by dispensational interpreters like John Hagee, Tim LaHaye, and Hal Lindsey is essentially a theology of despair and not hope. These apocalypticists don't appropriately grieve a self-mutilating world that cannot grasp its own plight; dispensationalism instills fatalism and resignation. In its darkest moments, dispensationalism exhibits a gleeful sense of triumphalism and cynical self-righteousness about those left behind. The fact that this theology has become the main understanding of the end times for millions is an indictment on Christianity.

Less easily understood is the way dispensationalism

THE ELDER

There should be an extra indictment for all solider-themed Vacation Bible School curricula.

---

flattens out the symbolic power of the Bible so that it no longer energizes our consciousness; it constricts our vision. We fail to see how revolutionary Revelation is in questioning our too-easy associations of God and the social order. God can be disruptive of all systems of oppression, and it's delusional on our part to assume that in the moment of unveiling we'll not discover that we've been doing the work of the beast. The God of Revelation is not easily domesticated into our systems of order or interpretation. Our willingness to use violence to secure ourselves, our desire to destroy others in order that we might prevail, even our inability to see that there are other possibilities than future destruction, situate us in hopelessness, not promise.

My introduction to the world of Rapture culture may have been fairly benign, but it exposed me to a world I might have easily dismissed as we often do with those who wear particleboard placards around their necks proclaiming the end is near. In this sense I was taken, caught up with wanting to know why people believe the things they do; how beliefs shape people's lives:

"And . . . did you find what you were looking for?" asks the nineteen-year-old.

"No, I still haven't found what I'm looking for," admits the older man.

"Give it a rest, Bono. Be serious for a minute. Do you grasp why people cling to the things they do?"

"We all cling to something, even if it's just our ego." The older one rubs his rapidly balding head. "I learned that from the Buddha as well as Jesus, but yes, I've come to understand that faith is something more important than waiting for The End. But I knew that at your age."

"Faith sounds like a buzzkill, dude, those millions constantly waiting for The End. But I see that it's part of the allure, the drama of it all. Nick Cage had me on the edge of my seat wondering if he'd land that plane."

"*Valley Girl* was better than that *Left Behind* dreck."

"Don't be hating."

"If The End, or even heaven for that matter, is all that Christianity's got, then it deserves to die. If God has determined the fate of the world already and we're only playing out the string, then we should shake our fists in God's face and refuse to play along."

"Whoa there ole' dude, dial it back a bit. Who pissed in your Cracklin' Oat Bran? Damn, you grew crusty in your old age. The End is infused in our consciousness; we can't escape it. It's not just Christians—Jews, Muslims, Hindus, Buddhists, most other religions ponder the final horizon. For many of them the world's destruction is the occasion for a new world, renewed and pure."

"That's just what worries me. You see the problem, right? That bright sparkly new world, the pure world where all enemies are vanquished, is a totalitarian hells-cape, devoid of ambiguity and because of that, full of violence."

"Not sure I follow you."

"Okay, stay with me here because I know you wander off at times. If the end-timers believe they're right about God, then that means they see themselves on God's side. They'll argue that it's God doing the killing at The End, only it won't be God trying to kill all the Muslims and Commies, or anyone else *they* deem God's enemies. They're the ones smashing homes and blowing stuff up, or cheerleading those who do, because in their minds, this is what God wants. How much more totalitarian can you get than to claim that your act of murder is God's will? Religious alchemists have been transmuting murder into piety for millennia."

"Old man take a look at my life; I'm a lot like you were."

"Bite me, Neil, and don't avoid the question. Have you seen anything in apocalypses that suggest that the enemy is also a human being, created by God and worthy of respect?"

"Uh, no, because in most apocalypses it's good vs. evil, light and dark."

"Right, which is why in the wrong hands apocalypses run the danger of totalitarianism. Life is not that simple, and to place ourselves constantly on the side of the angels is deception of the highest order. Speculation about the end times just ratchets this delusion up so we can feel righteous about following God while we destroy our enemies. That's not the gospel."

"Okay, point taken. I sorta knew this when I was in the Children of God, but is there anything life-affirming in apocalypses?"

"I read once that apocalypse is a journey from extinction to salvation. Maybe this is a way forward. As we move from darkness to light there is salvation, not just the loony parts people like to write about because it's click bait on their blogs."

Christ Has Died, Christ Has Risen, Christ Will Come Again

Christ has died. Christ has risen. Christ will come again. These are words repeated millions of times every week, words that echo over expectant, waiting congregations, but what are we to do with them? We're more comfortable with the first two proclamations than the third, wondering silently why these ancient words should be a part of our faith. *Christ will come again* confronts us with the inescapable reality that Christianity is an eschatological faith. If we think about it, however, this shouldn't surprise

us—human beings are inescapably eschatological creatures because our lives are limited. We're continually confronted in our own bodies with the shadows and anxieties
that whisper to us in moments of silence. Does life have
any meaning? Was there any purpose for my life other
than throwing my genetic code a bit further down the
field? We question if there's something hanging out there,
just beyond the lights on our porch, as we peer into the
darkness. It eludes our grasp; a thing we can sometimes
feel, but can't hold tightly. We secretly hope that it's not
all over when we die. We ponder The End, our end, every
waking moment, and Christianity responds with a simple,
yet profound truth: *Christ has died, Christ has risen, Christ
will come again.*

THE BISHOP

The more you
spiritualize and
individualize the
resurrection, the less it's
actually about God's work in Christ.

In these three short statements we find a story, a tale
of how much love exists in the universe, appearances to
the contrary. Love becomes flesh, shares embodiment with
all life in a way that is mysterious and profound. This love
ensures that death is neither the final word, nor the ultimate answer to our questions. Even though we hang on
the edges of uncertainty about what form that new life

will take, we're a resurrection people, mediating life to a world in love with its own destruction. As profound as the promise of resurrection is, however, *Christ will come again* has given birth to no small number of interesting, mesmerizing, frustrating, and terrifying expressions of The End.

Christ will come again has spawned massive destruction through the centuries, in no small part because some particular group of believers saw themselves as the saints who would help God wield that clarifying scythe at the end of days. Those who currently hold tightly to fantasies of the destruction of the earth, who secretly desire the burning of their enemies, even while they dream of escape from this wicked world, have many historical ancestors. But consuming fire and massive death are not the only ways we can think about the end times.

There's a rich diversity in Christianity that does allow for other images to inform and shape us. There is more than one way to think about The End.[1] For example, a word that we haven't used much to this point is the Greek word *telos*, meaning the goal or ends toward which we're moving. If *eschaton* is the end of all things, *telos* is the trajectory we're following to get there. Another way of putting this is to ask, toward what end are we moving? We could be moving to that conflagration written of in so many prophecy books, or perhaps something different.

Finally! Other options!!

THE ACOLYTE

Other traditions in Christianity pointed to the idea that God desires the world to become divine and this potential is embedded within material existence. Irenaeus believed that God's desire was that we were destined to grow into God and God was destined to grow into us, but this took vast amounts of time for God and humankind to become accustomed to one another. This idea did not become the main story of Christianity, though we might have saved ourselves a lot of problems if we had paid as much attention to this as we did to Augustine. If apocalypse is a journey from extinction to salvation and the end is a destination not yet fixed, we discover a world of possibilities, even within the accepted narrative of Christianity bequeathed to us by Augustine.

A Tale of Two Cities

When Augustine wrote *City of God*, he was probing this idea of the ends toward which we move. We saw earlier that he was responding to the charge that Rome had collapsed because the empire had stopped worshiping pagan gods in favor of the Christian one. He answered these charges with metaphors that situated the world poised between two cities: the Earthly City (Rome), and the City of God (Jerusalem). Rome (Babylon in John's telling and I'll use both these terms to make my argument) and Jerusalem constitute the realities that shape us until the end of time. These two entities manifest their own distinctive energies and we're enmeshed within them to such a degree it's sometimes hard to tell them apart.

The energies that animate Rome dominate and destroy all that which stands in Rome's way. In fact,

Augustine argued that the unconstrained state was little more than a massive crime syndicate, a concept not hard to entertain when looking at the powers in our age as they race blindly toward the oligarchy of the rich and powerful. Jerusalem, informed by a different set of virtues, orients itself differently than Rome. We can hear the echoes of the royal and prophetic consciousness in this dichotomy. The problem for the church is that sometimes Jerusalem mimics Rome, apes its desire for power, even though this is a distortion of what Jerusalem was meant for. It's often hard to tell the difference between the cities. This is where *telos* offers us occasions for discernment because it raises the question of ends. What are the goals that motivate our lives and what city are we investing in?

At this point you may be rightly suspicious of such a simplistic dualism. The world is a more complex place than to expect just two choices. The moral landscape we navigate is seldom so black and white, so stark, as to imply there are only two paths to choose. The muddled path of good and evil runs through every one of us. It's because of this tension we think we need the massive military of Rome to keep us from being overrun by the barbarians. If the poor and hungry have to sacrifice food and shelter so that they can be free, that's just the price they have to pay, right? Freedom costs, after all, and better the masters you know than the ones you don't. But freedom purchased at the expense of food and shelter is another form of enslavement.

These false choices (you're either with us or the evildoers) are the tactic of those throughout history who seek to control us. The promise to keep us safe is ultimately a fascist appeal; a paternalistic totalitarianism that says the state (Rome) is the only thing keeping the barbarians at bay. Caught between such a narrow range of choices,

THE ELDER

Shhh! Don't say that too loud. They are listening.

we're often unable to step back and acknowledge the desperation of others, the voices of those on the other side who may have legitimate moral claims.

If we consider ourselves residents of Jerusalem, however, we need to reflect on how we define ourselves in contrast to Rome or Babylon's appeal. We feel the pressure every day to conform to Rome's version of reality, to capitulate to the "wisdom" of peace through violence. Caught in the lure of totalitarian claims ("We'll keep you safe; we're the only ones who can in a world like this.") we live in a world so thin, so lacking in texture and moral imagination that we're only given two choices by our masters—accept our morality or die. It all feels so dead and sterile and not a choice at all. Is there escape from the clutches of Rome's rough beast slouching toward Jerusalem?[2]

The distinction between earthly and heavenly cities that Augustine made is not an easy dualism; it's more a question of which energies presently drive the world and the allegiances we give to them. This can be complex because sometimes Rome brings peace, sometimes Jerusalem brings pain and suffering; especially in its willingness to tell the truth to those who don't want to hear it. If we consider the larger material effects of these two orientations to the world, they can be tricky to sort out, because most of us make our home in Rome, though we often don't realize this.

Admitting you are complicit in the problem is the first step to addressing it.

THE BISHOP

The myth of your own purity is a defense mechanism that keeps your eyes from seeing the problem.

The best trick Rome has is making its account of the world seem inevitable, assumed, and never to be questioned. To exist in Rome means to accept reality on Rome's terms. To question the social orders that the empire builds, the ways in which human beings order their lives, is to blaspheme the sacred order the empire is built upon. Babylon polices the boundaries of our imagination in the desire to force us into its constricted field of vision. *This* is the meaning of the beast—the beast is the heart of all orders that exist to maintain their own power over against the life that God desires for God's people, a life that opposes the energies of the beast.

In Jerusalem we exist within the story of God's creation moving to consummation, but the end of all things is the New Jerusalem where neither the claims of Babylon, nor the temple as symbol of political power, belong. While we're constantly on pilgrimage, the continuing process of promise, unfaithfulness, judgment, and redemption is never removed from our very human struggle to continually create the world. The obligations we have to ourselves, to others, to God, are never over, even to the end of the age. These relationships take shape in the tensions between Rome and Jerusalem.

This brings us to the door of suspicion once more, for we have been told as postmoderns to suspect metanarratives, stories that exercise a totalizing control over our lives. As much as I resist being shoved into a story that doesn't fit, life itself is a metanarrative. Life carries its own dynamic, ebbing and flowing between promise and peril, a swirling mass of energies we cannot escape. If we're lucky we get to contribute in writing our own story, but if we're caught under Rome's wheels, ground into the dust of serving Rome and its masters, we're powerless to write our lives, existing instead in the endless monotony of feeding the beast that rules over us.

Even as people of faith we often find ourselves oscillating between Rome and Jerusalem, never quite able to escape Rome's demands, always finding Jerusalem's hope a fingertip away. If we're honest, we wonder which city shapes us more. We instinctually know that the citizens of Jerusalem should bring relief and, yes, salvation to those who live under the boot of Rome, but we're often at a loss for how to do that.

Earthly empires rule by kings, presidents, and prime ministers, some of whom are benign, many of whom use fear and repression to keep people cowed and obedient. Orders are instituted in the state to ensure loyalty. Oaths are called for; obedience to the rulers is demanded, and we saw in Samuel's warning to Israel what happens when you give yourselves to a king. They'll exploit you for their own glory; build temples that lock God into supporting political orders that ignore the prophets. This is what Rome/Babylon does. It consumes all things in its path, turning them into fuel to sustain itself. It becomes a self-perpetuating machine that must exploit the resources of people, land, and wealth to maintain itself. According to Revelation, we're so enmeshed within this demonic energy we have become blind to the fact that the merchants of the world, the job creators, traffic in human lives (Revelation 18:13).

But the spirit of Jerusalem prophesies against secular and religious legitimation of oppression to give another answer to the suffering of the world. We find a hint of how Jerusalem constitutes itself in Revelation. Of striking importance is the fact that in the New Jerusalem, John tells us, "I did not see a temple in the city, because the Lord God Almighty and the Lamb are its temple" (Revelation 21:22). Given how much energy is being presently being put into the rebuilding of the third temple in Jerusalem, it should give us pause that for many biblical authors the temple is unimportant at the end of all things. The ambiguity concerning the temple that runs through the scripture reflects our preoccupations, not God's desire. Those who are unconcerned with the costs in death and destruction of their desire to drive Muslims off the Temple Mount have become so captive to an interpretation of faith they are blind to the fact that their heart lives in Babylon, not Jerusalem.

Sheep or Goats?

When we contemplate the apocalypse we can think differently about the end of the world, because The End is not necessarily what apocalypses were written for. Apocalypses speak to the end of corrupt and oppressive regimes. The New Jerusalem, while postponed, makes itself present in our midst, a counternarrative to the story of Babylon/Rome. Because we know the hope embedded within the story, we can see ourselves as something other than prisoners in a decayed and fallen world, futilely wandering the wilderness waiting for our redemption. Salvation does not happen at the end of a distant cataclysm; salvation is a present reality, meant to shape our lives in this world.

The dramatic accounts of Christ's return we read about in dispensationalism often resonate with us because we suspect that nothing other than a cleansing flood of God's wrath can sweep away the vast amounts of brokenness and pain we encounter daily on our computer screens or in newspapers. The biblical writers probably felt the same way. For example, in Matthew's renderings of The End the choices are stark at the final judgment.

The parable of the sheep and goats may be instructive for us as we think about The End. This parable, found in Matthew 25, comes after the "small apocalypse" we looked at earlier. Matthew follows his account of the apocalypse with three parables. These stories are interesting, given that Matthew places them right after Jesus tells the disciples about the final days. The parable of the bridesmaids (Matthew 25:1–13) speaks to the necessity for patient and prepared waiting for the bridegroom, even when it seems like the time has passed. The parable of the talents

(Matthew 25:14–30) cautions us in how we use our gifts while we wait for the return of the master. The third parable is the judgment of the nations at the end of the world, and surprises us with a thing we often overlook in our fascination with the apocalypse.

In this story, when the Son of Man comes in glory, the nations (and just a word here; if you were to read this as the judgment of the nations instead of individuals, it would look a lot different) are gathered before him and he separates them into sheep and goats. ("Yay, stupid goats are finally gonna get what's coming to 'em.") The sheep inherit the kingdom because they fed the hungry, gave drink to the thirsty, clothed the naked, visited those in prison, and took care of the sick. The goats, braying loudly, are all: "We never saw you rooting around in trash cans behind grocery stores late at night, and besides, those in prison deserved it, especially the ones we executed (#KellyGissendaner). You couldn't have been there. We never saw you sick because we made sure our politicians wouldn't allow the poor in our hospitals, and don't get us started on immigrants. You couldn't have been with them because they broke our laws. How were we to know it was you?" And the Son of Man breaks through this self-righteousness to say, "You knew because I told you; you just cared more for yourselves than you did my children, your own brothers and sisters" (Matthew 25:31–46).

Where do we stand in this story? Matthew's parables challenge us with the virtues that shape the New Jerusalem. He's unconcerned with golden streets, jeweled adornment, and measured cities (Revelation 21). Perhaps we're uncomfortable with Matthew's take on The End because it smacks of works righteousness. It should be sobering to realize, however, that in Matthew's vision of The End, when the nations are judged, how we lived our lives, the things we gave ourselves to, matters. Salvation in the face of extinction means very specific actions are done throughout all of our lives, and the beginning of our endings is found in courageous acts of inclusion.

THE ELDER

Was anyone else anticipating a Matthew 25 ending? I bet every progressive has that text underlined in every color of the rainbow. Oh and Luke 4.

As much as I hate to admit this, in Matthew the eschatological is an ethical moment. The great revelation in this passage, however, is that at the end of time we find Christ never left; he was always present. Christ confronts us in the needs of the world, the hungry, the dispossessed, and the imprisoned—in all those who live on the margins. Christ meets us in the face of those whom Rome (sometimes with Jerusalem's goading) has used as fodder for its will to power. In those moments when we allow the New Jerusalem and not Rome/Babylon to shape us, we become agents of grace in a broken world. Rejection of Rome means we attend to the victims of the state, even as those victims grow more numerous. Babylon has acquired a voracious appetite for feeding on the vulnerable and weak, and it gorges now on the poor without mercy. The faces of those needing water, bread, and freedom are diverse and numerous because the world of massive need is the world that Babylon has created, even as its tentacles reach out to enslave yet more.

In this brutal reality what does it mean for us to say Christ will come again? We have need of Christ now, not later. Christ comes again in our willingness to manifest the life of God, a life of suffering love, within Babylon. This isn't as sexy or exciting as the *Left Behind* books where the Tribulation Force jets around the globe to watch the destruction of the world. The appeal of a story that calls us to sacrifice our egos and agendas pales in comparison to one where our enemies are put under our feet and we reign triumphant. Christ coming again requires the discipline to resist the allure of Babylon every waking moment. Resistance to Rome/Babylon, and the manifestation of mercy and grace under Rome's pressure, is how the apocalypse becomes salvation instead of extinction.

The resistance I'm speaking of is not one that rises up in violence against Rome; it's not the violence of taking land or possessions because you believe God commanded it. To resist doesn't mean lashing out when the world we have constructed around our prejudices and hatreds falls before us like a lowered flag. It means positioning ourselves with the most vulnerable of society, the ones whom the powerful disparage and manipulate. We don't want to find ourselves standing with those who weep over Babylon's fall. They mourn the loss of their power to buy and sell human lives, the ability to fashion the world after their own desires.

Christ comes again through our willingness to make God's grace a living reality. This means that we'll have to embrace different disciplines than the ones Rome offers. As we turn toward the future we have a promise of something new arriving. This hope of the new flies in the face of the popular eschatologies today that envision the future as nothing other than destruction, desolation, and massive death.

We live caught in the competing visions of Rome and Jerusalem. A quick survey of the morning news reveals a confused and conflicted world stumbling through darkness. Violence is our default strategy for getting what we want, and we're intent on making sure that the earth cannot sustain life at anything more than a subsistence level. Any observant person sees we live in perilous times, which explains the attraction of LaHaye, Lindsey, and the rest of their ilk who believe the world rockets toward Armageddon.

False consciousness and bad interpretation shouldn't sway us. We can escape being held captive by the fictions of end time hucksters and their story of doomed humanity because of the hope that God is present in the darkness. Dietrich Bonhoeffer wrote from his prison cell that we live in the world as if God did not exist. This is a hard but important truth to grasp, and yet it is not entirely negative. Bonhoeffer believed that the further we move into the world, immersing ourselves within its sufferings and joys, the more we move into the life of God. If the future exists as a horizon of hope, extending itself to us in promise and potential, then our immersion into this world is the calling of God. Caught in the tension between Rome/Babylon and Jerusalem we have to choose. One of those cities leads to exclusion, suffering, and continuing death;

the other leads to embrace and a fierce burning desire to make whole the broken places.[3]

Apocalypses offer us many visions of a richly imagined future, but there is a theme that we can pick out amidst the diversity, and, yes, I know this is an outrageous claim. We're called to be light, shared with all life. In the midst of great darkness, the gospel calls us to incarnate in our stumbling imperfect ways the presence of God. The gospel challenges us to manifest in our very lives the promise of reconciliation and peace to those who would kill to protect "God's space."

Christ comes again every time we choose love over hatred, peace over war, feeding the hungry over sending in drones, and resisting those who whisper in our ear that we must be "realistic" about the world even as they assiduously work to tear it apart. Christ comes again every moment we have the courage to make known the rumors of glory (#brucecockburn). In a world poised on the edge of massive violence we can become defined by visions of apocalyptic terror, our imaginations taken prisoner by peculiar interpretations of biblical texts; or we can embrace the vision that in the midst of this present uncertainty, Christ is the future coming towards us, seeking to draw us and the world into God's grace.

The End

Notes

Chapter 1

1. Amy Johnson Frykholm, *Rapture Culture: Left Behind in Evangelical America* (New York: Oxford University Press, 2004). Frykholm offers a measured and sensitive portrayal of those who hold to ideas about the imminent return of Jesus, showing how this anticipation of Christ's return provides meaning and purpose in the lives of believers.

2. http://pressreleases.religionnews.com/2013/09/11/shock-poll-startling-numbers-of-americans-believe-world-now-in-the-end-times/. Last accessed December 21, 2015.

3. http://publicreligion.org/research/2014/11/believers-sympathizers-skeptics-americans-conflicted-climate-change-environmental-policy-science/#.VYl5O6YkweM. Last accessed September 4, 2015.

4. See, for example, Paul Boyer, *When Time Shall Be No More: Prophecy Belief in American Culture* (Cambridge, MA: Harvard University Press, 1990). This book is a comprehensive look at the way prophecy belief has influenced America, but its historical focus extends back to apocalyptic literature and the early church.

5. Matthew Avery Sutton, *American Apocalypse: A History of Modern Evangelicalism* (Cambridge, MA: Belknap, 2014), 355.

6. Sutton, 370.

7. Sutton, 346.

Chapter 2

1. Craig C. Hill, *In God's Time: The Bible and the Future* (Grand Rapids, MI: Eerdmans, 2002), 86–92.

2. See Charles Taylor's *A Secular Age* (Cambridge, MA: Belknap, 2007) for an account of the vast power our constructions of the world exercise over us through time.

3. John J. Collins, *The Apocalyptic Imagination: An Introduction to Jewish Apocalyptic Literature* (Grand Rapids, MI: Eerdmans, 1984), 26. Collins is considered one of the foremost scholars in apocalyptic literature and is worth getting to know if you want to burrow a bit deeper into all of this.

4. Hill, 101.

5. Hal Lindsey, with C. C. Carlson, *The Late Great Planet Earth* (Grand Rapids, MI: Zondervan, 1970), 91.

6. Collins, 94.

7. See Collins's discussion of this, pp. 101–4. He makes a convincing case that Daniel is referring to Michael the archangel in this passage.

8. Collins, 113.

Chapter 3

1. Gerd Theissen, *Gospel in Context: Social and Political History in the Synoptic Tradition* (Minneapolis: Fortress Press, 1992), 157, 164.

2. Hill, 155.

3. Collins, 263.

4. Collins, 264.

Chapter 4

1. Barbara Rossing, *The Rapture Exposed: The Message of Hope in the Book of Revelation* (New York: Basic Books, 2004), 104–6.

2. http://marshill.se/marshill/media/doctrine/kingdom-god-reigns /thug-jesus. Last accessed October 24, 2015.

3. Craig R. Koester, *Revelation and the End of All Things* (Grand Rapids, MI: Eerdmans, 2001), 118.

4. M. Eugene Boring, *Revelation* (Louisville: John Knox, 1989), 151.

5. Koester, 118.

6. Koester, 130–31.

7. See, for example, *The New Interpreter's Bible*, vol. 12 (Nashville: Abingdon, 1995), 659.

8. See, for example Lynn Huber's work on Revelation, *Thinking and Seeing with Women in Revelation* (London: Bloomsbury T. & T. Clark, 2015), as well as her earlier work, *Like a Bride Adorned: Reading Metaphor in John's Apocalypse* (London: Bloomsbury T. & T. Clark, 2007). See also Tina Pippin, *Death and Desire: The Rhetoric of Gender in the Apocalypse of John* (Louisville: Westminster John Knox, 1992). These are only a couple of books that critique how gender is framed in Revelation. If you really want to geek out and explore race, gender, empire, and Revelation, take a look at Shanell T. Smith, *The Woman Babylon and the Marks of the Empire: Reading Revelation with a Postcolonial Womanist Hermeneutics of Ambivelence* (Minneapolis: Fortress Press, 2014).

Chapter 5

1. Bernard McGinn, ed., *The Encyclopedia of Apocalypticism, Vol. II, Apocalypticism in Western History and Culture* (New York: Continuum, 1999), 23. These volumes are an excellent introduction to the historical and biblical complexity of this subject and should be considered great resources for understanding the history of apocalypticism.

2. McGinn, 31.

3. McGinn, 32.

4. Boyer, 49.

5. McGinn, 292.

6. Boyer, 70.

7. For an interesting experiment go to Google images and type in "The Great Disappointment." The maps, headlines, pictures, prophecy charts, and other interesting artifacts gives you a sense of what this looked like back in the day.

8. Sutton, 31.

9. Sutton, 141–43.

Chapter 6

1. http://www.theatlantic.com/international/archive/2014/11/the-dangers-on-the-temple-mount/382787/. Last accessed October 26, 2015. You can also do a search and find more up-to-date material, but this is a good primer for what's at stake.

2. http://www.beliefnet.com/Faiths/Christianity/End-Times/On-The-Road-To-Armageddon.aspx?p=1. Last accessed October 25, 2015. Though a bit dated, Timothy Weber gives a judicious

account of how Israel worked to court evangelical Christians into political action that would support Israel unconditionally.

3. Boyer, 186.

4. Lindsey, 54.

5. http://www.leftbehind.com/02_end_times/ultimatesign.asp. Last accessed October 24, 2015.

6. Rossing, 51.

7. Gershom Gorenberg, *The End of Days: Fundamentalism and the Struggle for the Temple Mount* (Oxford: Oxford University Press, 2000), 11.

8. Gorenberg, 8ff.

9. https://www.templeinstitute.org. Last accessed October 24, 2015.

10. This is a complex history that defies easy separation of "good" and "bad." Some sources for further study are Itamar Rabinovitch's *Waging Peace: Israel and the Arabs, 1948-2003* (Princeton: Princeton University Press, 2004); Charles D. Smith, *Palestine and the Arab-Israeli Conflict: A History with Documents*, 7th edition (Boston and New York: Bedford/St. Martin's, 2009); and Sami Adwan, Dan Bar-On, Eyal Naveh, and Peace Research Institute in the Middle East (PRIME), eds., *Side by Side: Parallel Histories of Israel-Palestine* (New York: New Press, 2012).

11. Rossing, 75.

12. Lindsey, 80.

13. http://www.leftbehind.com/02_end_times/ultimatesign.asp. Last accessed October 24, 2015.

14. Rossing, 71.

15. http://www.leftbehind.com/02_end_times/threesigns.asp. Last accessed October 24, 2015.

16. Boyer, 204.

17. Gorenberg, 165.

18. Gorenberg, 141.

19. Boyer, 213.

20. Boyer, 127.

Chapter 8

1. http://www.haaretz.com/news/israel/.premium-1.661848. Last accessed October 24, 2015.

2. Robert Bellah, *Religion in Human Evolution: From the Paleolithic to the Axial Age* (Cambridge, MA: Belknap, 2011), 287. See also Karen Armstrong, *Fields of Blood: Religion and the History*

of Violence (New York: Alfred A. Knopf, 2014), for an account of Israel's beginnings.

3. Walter Brueggemann, *The Prophetic Imagination*, 2nd edition (Minneapolis: Fortress Press, 2001).

4. Bellah, 298.

5. Armstrong, 113–14.

6. Brueggemann, 25.

7. Bellah, 298.

Chapter 9

1. Chief among modern theologians who called attention to the inescapable nature of Christianity as an eschatological faith is Jürgen Moltmann. His book *Theology of Hope* (Minneapolis: Fortress Press, 1993) is a twentieth-century classic, pointing out that Christian faith lives on the boundaries of a hope that transcends circumstances, that defeats death (or, as Steven Colbert might say, "deathiness"), leading us to embrace hope as a guiding theological category. Moltmann continues his insightful take on this with a later volume, *The Coming of God: Christian Eschatology* (Minneapolis: Augsburg Fortress, 1996).

2. #WilliamButlerYeats, "The Second Coming." And, yes, I know it's Bethlehem instead of Jerusalem, but I'm riffing on Augustine.

3. One of Miroslav Volf's greatest contributions to contemporary theology is his book *Exclusion and Embrace: A Theological Exploration of Identity, Otherness, and Reconciliation* (Nashville: Abingdon, 1996).